COMPASS

NAVIGATING YOUR
TEAM FORWARD

SPENCER
NORDYKE

COMPASS

NAVIGATING YOUR
TEAM FORWARD

SPENCER
NORDYKE

N-COMPASS: *Navigating Your Team Forward*
by Spencer Nordyke

Published by Blaze Publishing House
www.blazepublishinghouse.com
BPH is a division of Ministry Solutions, LLC
Mansfield, TX 76063
info@BlazePublishingHouse.com

Due to the multiple versions of the Bible used in this book, they are listed in the back of the book.

Copy Editor - Kent Booth
Editor - Laura-Lee Booth
Cover design - Ryan Nordyke
Prepared for Publication - Ministry Solutions, LLC

ISBN-13: 978-1-883442-01-9

BPH

*I dedicate this book to the generations of young men and women who have come alongside me throughout the years of ministry and have helped hold up my hands—the bands, the interns, the concerts, the camps, the conventions, the traveling teams, and those who listened to me preach whether just one time or week-in and week-out. I want to say, "Thank you!" for your dedication, your hard work, and the way you gave of yourselves to help shape the lives of others in **Reaching Nations & Generations!***

And especially to both of my sons, Jesse and Ryan Nordyke, who have traveled countless hours on the road with us, have been to more youth camps than I care to admit, and have stayed in more hotel rooms than most people ever will. "Thank you!" for giving your teenage and college years to help pioneer Youth WAVE Church and become generational leaders impacting your world today! You are both perfect examples of modern-day disciples of Jesus! I am a grateful dad!

To all of you who have become pastors, doctors, lawyers, business-men and women, store owners, moms and dads, and those who have taken the essence of the leadership of Jesus into your circles of influence, I am so proud of who you are and what you are producing in this next generation. This book speaks of your involvement in this leadership journey! May God bless all the work of your hands!

ACKNOWLEDGMENTS

Special thanks to Ryan Nordyke who designed the cover and patiently walked through this experience with me. I value your immense creativity and your amazing eye for design. You are the best!

Thanks to my dad, Carleton L. Nordyke, for helping me to sort out our ancestry and for passing on the Nordyke name for future generations who will cross their ocean to a new land!

I want to thank Victoria Austin for her hard work and input on this book. Thank you for your friendship and encouragement and your prayers and faith in this project.

Special appreciation goes out to Tina Thomas Photography for the great work creating the pictures. You know what we like!

This book would not have been possible without Kent and Laura-Lee Booth who have a passion for writing, producing, and publishing books. You have made me be a better writer by asking all the right questions. "Thank you!" for the hours of input, expertise, advice, and hanging out together over Mexican food. You are true examples of being life-long friends!

Most of all, I want to thank my beautiful wife who literally labored over this book with me. I could not have done this without you, Cyndy! We are living the adventure!

WHAT PEOPLE ARE SAYING ABOUT . . .
N-COMPASS:
NAVIGATING YOUR TEAM FORWARD!

"I have been blessed beyond words to have a front row seat my entire life and witness Spencer's immeasurable guidance and leadership abilities. His gift of applying biblical leadership principles to everyday life has personally impacted me as a father, leader, and successful businessman. I am so excited about this book and know that the personal, real life stories, scripture-based guidance, and practical applications will be a great tool in helping you navigate the journey."

Jesse Nordyke, Son

"This book is so awesome; I wish I would have written it! N-Compass: Navigating Your Team Forward, is a must-read for every leader at every level. In a day when we are starving because of a lack of leadership, this book is God-sent. Spencer and Cyndy Nordyke have written a precise, easy-to-read tool that will sharpen us all. I endorse this book 100% and hold the authors in high esteem."

Josh M. Barclay, Mark Barclay Ministries

"This book will help improve and sharpen you as a person and a leader. I highly recommend it to you and your team!"

Rocky Tannehill, Entrepreneur

"Wow! Wow! Wow! This is absolutely one of the greatest team formulas I have read since John Maxwell came onto the scene. I want to teach this to my staff and interns. You are amazing! You have never lost that anointing to instruct and direct leaders out of their potentials, instead of their failures. You da man!"

Steve Munds, Founder & Director of Go Ministries

"What a refreshing and innovative way to share the Word with your team! Spencer Nordyke's creativity shines again, as he takes life's day-to-day happenings and uses them to illustrate the power of God's Word in our lives."

Chris Mitchell, Pastor & Lifetime Friend

*"Spencer Nordyke's new book, **N-Compass**, is creative, thought-provoking and simply outstanding! Just like a compass is a navigational instrument used to accurately locate a position to establish a clear direction in moving forward to a desired destination, this book is a resourceful tool to sharpen leaders with a directional starting point to help move them and their teams forward as they pursue a Christ-centered mission! I highly recommend **N-Compass**. It will N-hance your personal life and your team."*

Ron Jutze
Ron Jutze Ministries

*"**N-Compass** fills readers with hope and motivation and challenges them to look at their dreams through God's lenses and reflect on their true calling. Spencer draws from his own experiences with friends, family, and reflections from his various ministry trips around the world, resulting in a personal and vulnerable account of the author's own spiritual journey, grounded in biblical principles with practical examples."*

Pastor Anthony Does
Ontario, Canada

"I am totally N-spired by my friend Spencer Nordyke's challenges in this book. Every believer ought to read it and pass it on to their friends and their pastors. Spencer not only writes it well on paper... He practices it well in his ministry and his life!"

Pastor Jerry Davis
Embassy Church – Disaster Pastor Network

"Spencer Nordyke has done it again. He has produced an extremely creative and informative ministry tool to help us all navigate through the varied waters of our lives. Well done!"

Pastor George Pearsons
Eagle Mountain International Church
Kenneth Copeland Ministries

"Spencer and Cyndy Nordyke are two of the best navigators I know when it comes to leadership and ministry. I'm confident their new book will charge and challenge you with creative biblical insights to get you and your team moving in the right direction. When running low on leadership creativity and facing a bad case of vision block, you'll find N-Compass to be a very present help in times of trouble."

Pastor Brad Howard
Lakeshore Church - Rockwall, Texas

"I love Spencer and Cyndy's passion and heart for the coming generations. Their enthusiasm is contagious; their knowledge, deep; their wisdom, practical. Invest this book into yourself and others."

Pastor Brian Leifeste
Northpoint Church - New Braunfels, Texas

"Spencer and Cyndy Nordyke are gifted communicators who have been used by God to train and equip leaders whose ministries now span the globe. One of their unique gifts has been captured in this book: the ability to take common words and phrases and transform them into truly catalytic inspiration-generators. A read through this book will line your leadership warehouse with insights and concepts that will enhance your ability to communicate and cast inspirational vision to those you lead."

Dr. David & Cheree' Wright
Lead Pastors, LifeLinkChurch.com

"I am excited about this book. Just the fact that you are reading it convinces me that there are people who are passionate about raising up the next generation of leaders. That is exactly the kind of passion you will notice in Spencer and Cyndy Nordyke. They are truly gifted at training next-generation leaders, and this book is a creative way to help you N-ergize your passion as well."

Eric Partin, Pastor
Shoreline Church
Destin and Fort Walton Beach, Florida

"With our 15 years in youth ministry, I would highly recommend this book for the youth leader today. It places a 'handle' on some of the ideas we would all like to teach and convey to today's youth. Again, I think this can be a great tool as a supplement to a regular teaching curriculum or as a stand-alone teaching guide."

Louie Caraveo, Associate Pastor
Redeemer Christian Fellowship
Master Builders Construction - Midland, Texas

"We have known Spencer and Cyndy Nordyke for years, and the word that most sums up their gift to the Body of Christ is 'encouragement!' Spending time with them personally or reading their words on a page, you suddenly remember who you have been created to be in Christ Jesus, and you feel empowered again to accomplish whatever great tasks the Lord has set before you. We cannot wait to see this book release the anointing that they have carried for years further than ever before."

Cleetus & Nichole Adrian, Founding Pastors
Deliverance Bible Church International,
Directors of MK1615 Mission and Missionaries to France

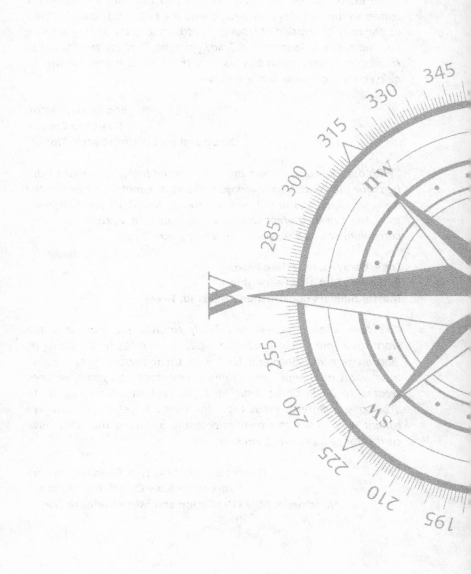

CONTENTS

N-TRODUCTION

H ere I am, Spencer Nordyke, sitting in Nordstrom's coffee shop at Northeast Mall close to North Richland Hills, Texas (which, by the way, is in North Texas)—a very fitting place to write the introduction to the *N-COMPASS* book! Obviously, a theme is already starting to develop here—the letter "N"—and it's very directional. If there is one thing I have found to be true, it is this: Having the right direction in life is crucial to success. We all need help, at times, navigating our way forward.

After 36 years of preaching, teaching, pastoring, training, traveling, and living life, I feel as if I have started ministry all over again. Some might call it a mid-life crisis or some type of ministry rebound, but neither is correct. It is simply a matter of God revealing a new direction for me. All that I have experienced has now brought me to this place of pioneering once again. This is something my family and I have done many, many times before; however, this time it is with a new spiritual depth that Cyndy and I didn't possess when we were young and just starting out. Back then, it was just us and blind faith. Even then, God was navigating our steps.

I can still remember the excitement we felt in one of our early adventures. God gave us specific instructions and said, "I want you to go to Tyler, TX and help raise up a Christian teaching center." We were so excited to know God had spoken to us, but there was one major challenge—we didn't know a soul in Tyler, TX at the time! Nevertheless, we stepped out with only what we could stuff in our two-door Cutlass Supreme and headed to Tyler. When we arrived, Cyndy saw in the local paper that a prophetess named Beth Alves was speaking at a local church on the subject, "What God wants for Tyler!" We quickly decided to attend that meeting, because we knew God had positioned us to be a part of whatever was about to happen there.

Before the evening service started, the host pastor's wife introduced herself and asked Cyndy where we were from. Cyndy told her we were moving from Dallas. The pastor's wife then asked, "Have you ever heard of Christ for the Nations Institute?" Cyndy quickly responded, "Yes, we graduated from there." "What do you guys do?" the pastor's wife asked. Cyndy replied, "We work with children and youth." Immediately, this lady turned to her husband (the senior pastor) and yelled, "THEY'RE HERE! THEY'RE HERE!" Cyndy and I looked at each other with the "Okay??" look, as we were not quite sure what, "They're here," exactly meant. We were about to find out.

It seems that three ladies in this church had been praying and fasting for three days. The focus of their fasting and prayer? For God to send them a young couple from Christ for the Nations to work with their children and youth! And we just showed up out of seemingly nowhere. Can you say, "Navigate"? To make a long story short, we served at that church for 18 months and it was one of the most intense growing experiences of our lives. We learned so much from world-class leaders in the middle of East Texas. We were amazed at how God orchestrated all of that, but little did we know it was only the beginning of a life-long journey of God-filled navigations. Many of those stories are shared throughout this book.

Now, we are standing on the edge again with clear direction from the Lord, saying, "Write the vision." Just when we thought we were done pioneering, it's like we are starting all over again.

I was born in '56 and just turned 56 years old. I'm sure that has some significance on some cosmic level, but I still feel so young. I feel like a well-preserved '56 Thunderbird, (a personal favorite), and I'm getting ready to take this '56 out for a spin to see what it can do! Since Abraham started when he was 75 years old and Moses started at 80, I suppose I'm just the new kid on the block. Even at 56, I feel so much excitement and anticipation for what God is getting ready to do in our lives, and I know it's going to be the best chapter so far!

A LIFE OF JOURNEYS

From that time in Tyler until now, Cyndy and I have been on one constant journey with God. Sometimes, it has seemed as if we were on the highest mountain top in the world; while other times, we would look at each other and feel like God had forsaken us. Of course, He never has; but it sure seemed that way a few times. No matter what the circumstance, we have always—and will always—walk on His path.

I've often wondered why this pioneering, journeyman

spirit is deep within me. As God began to deal with me about writing this book, I began to search out some things from my ancestry and what I found answered a lot of questions.

Both my mother and my father's ancestors are from the Netherlands. My great-grandfather, Adrian Nordyke, set out for America in 1889 on *Holland America Lines' SS Rotterdam*. He sailed from Rotterdam, Netherlands to New York, probably in steerage class, which must have been a frightening journey for a 25-year-old farm worker who had never been anywhere in his life. The conditions on the steamships of that era were not at all like today. They were large rooms filled with bunk beds that had burlap mattresses stuffed with hay or seaweed, a life preserver that doubled as a pillow, and a tin pail with utensils for your meals—whatever kind of stew the crew would concoct—which were served from a giant vat. The 12 to 15 days of rocking back and forth in the belly of a giant metal tub would be an experience you would not soon forget. I wonder if he had to sleep with one eye open to keep anyone from stealing his meager belongings. Sharing that small space with hundreds of other people from many different nations was probably a challenging initiation for surviving in the new world!

He arrived on March 15, 1889, just two years after the Statue of Liberty was dedicated. I'm sure this was an amazing sight for him to see. My great-grandfather was then processed at Clinton Castle, formerly Fort Clinton, named for one of the mayors of New York. Ellis Island was not built for immigration into the U. S. until 1892. Four hundred years earlier, this spot was Fort Amsterdam when the city was called New Amsterdam in the New Netherlands Territory.

(This was before the Duke of York rallied the British troops and took over Manhattan Island, thus calling it New York, New York.) There must have been some roots of Dutch destiny there.

Adrian Nordyke then made his way to Grand Rapids, Michigan, where he met my great-grandmother, Jacoba Cora Mieras, who had arrived from Holland before he did. She came across the pond with her parents at 18 years old on a Red Star Line's ship. She arrived before the Statue of Liberty was erected. They traveled to western Michigan, settling not far from Holland and Zeeland, Michigan, where many Dutch families had made their new homes. By 1892 Adrian and Cora were married and ended up having 10 children. Their youngest boy, Dennis, was my grandfather.

And so, the Nordyke journey had begun.

Obviously this is not a book on my family history; however, at this moment, I feel much like my ancestors did—that we are on the greatest adventure of our lives! Today, we are back to how we started . . . with just Cyndy and I. Our two sons and their wives have given us seven beautiful grandchildren. There are now 13 of us altogether. I feel we have done our part in replenishing the earth, so now it's on to the new adventure. Through the years, one thing I have learned about launching out into something different is this: Every new adventure brings a new level of required trust. When you move to another level of life or ministry, you must establish a greater dependence on God for His divine direction and leadership.

Anything less will get you off course.

GOD'S GPS

Over the years, Cyndy and I have driven more miles across this country than either of us want to remember. It wasn't until recently that we decided to finally buy a Garmin GPS for our road trips. We thought this would be an easy way to find our way while traveling, but that proved not to be so easy after all. The learning curve on how to use the crazy thing was bigger than we anticipated. I thought you just plugged it in, and it told you where to go. NO! First, you have to read the instructions and then follow them.

It didn't take me long to figure out that every GPS system—even though they do the same thing—all work differently. For example, ours had different voice options. We decided to choose the racecar driver voice, so we could get to where we were going faster! The only problem was that this voice would come on at random times and say things like, "WATCH OUT! You have a diesel truck in your blind spot!" It was so annoying, so we went back to the instructions and chose a very soothing female voice that not only tells you when to turn, but includes all the street names; so you can avoid making directional mistakes that keep you going in circles.

This whole Garmin experience got me to thinking. Wouldn't it be great to have a God GPS system? I mean, how easy would it be if I could simply input, "Find Spencer and Cyndy's destiny," and then push, "GO!" Wouldn't that be wonderful? That GPS would give us turn-by-turn instructions on where to go, what roads to take, how far to travel before exiting, and how long it would take to reach the destination of "Destiny." This amazing tool would give us complete directions, so we wouldn't walk in circles for years and years.

Oh, if it were just that easy!

Many times, as leaders, we try to figure things out as we go. (Don't sit there and shake your head in disbelief; you know it's true!) The problem is that we do not take time to read the instructions to know what we are doing along the way. Instead, we listen to voices and opinions that give us random instructions about things which have nothing to do with our destiny. The results? We end up circling mountains that waste our time and energy. Now more than ever, we need the leadership of the Holy Spirit to get where He desires for us to be. And, we need each other's help and encouragement to encompass us with support for the journey.

HEAD NORTH

If there were ever a group of people who could've benefited from a spiritual GPS, it was the children of Israel in the Old Testament. When God delivered His people from the bondage of Egypt, they turned an 11-day journey into a 40-year spectacle. I would say they were directionally challenged, wouldn't you? After many years of wandering, they finally got this directive from God:

> *"And the Lord spake to me saying, 'You have compassed this mountain long enough, turn northward.'"*
>
> **Deuteronomy 2:2-3 (KJV)**

Isn't it amazing that God's specific direction to a very lost and misguided bunch was to head north? He could've said, "Go East," or, "Go to that tree over there and turn right," or even, "Go West, young man!" But, He specifically said, "Turn North." How interesting. I believe the reason God's specified this directive was because North is a constant directional navigation point that shows the way for those who are lost. Sure, it's nice to know where you are going; but to start a journey, you need a point of reference—somewhere to begin that puts the whole picture in perspective.

North is that reference point.

Look on any map, and you will find an "**N**." That's where **NORTH** is, and it puts the rest of the map in perspective. Look on a compass, and you will find an "**N**." **NORTH** defines where everything else is. Look up at night, and you can find the Big Dipper, which points to the end of the handle in the Little Dipper; and you'll find the **NORTH** Star, or Polaris. When you know where **NORTH** is, you automatically know where East, West, and South are; so you don't get lost—even in the dark! (Now, if no one ever taught you how to read a map, or use a compass, you might still be lost out there somewhere!)

Mariners crossing the Atlantic Ocean relied heavily on celestial navigation. Many times, they found their way by looking up at the **NORTH** Star and getting their bearings for the trip. This is vitally important when there are no landmarks, just hundreds of miles of water. Imagine Christopher Columbus crossing an ocean in a time when everyone else thought the world was flat and that if they went too far, they might fall off the edge of the earth! He knew that God was calling him to sail West across the waters to a new land, and knew he had to complete his mission even if no one else believed him! He had direction, he acted on it, and he discovered new lands. He knew where **NORTH** was.

On a quick personal note, you can imagine how intrigued I was to find out how my last name fits into all of this. It seems that the name "Nordyke" actually means, "North of the dyke." Now, every time I see or say or write my name, I'm looking at "North," and I thank God for His divine direction and hand on my life.

But the good news is no matter what your name is, you can live your life under God's provisional direction and know that He is not only the author and finisher of your faith, but that He will also provide direction for every step of the way.

If you're lost, find **NORTH**.

LEADERSHIP!

After mentoring several generations of young leaders, Cyndy and I find ourselves with a boatload of experiences. Some might contain keys which will help you and your team cross your ocean and settle into a new place of fulfillment. It's amazing when we get a note from one of those young disciples that says, "Thank you. You changed my life. You believed in me when I couldn't believe in myself." That is more rewarding than just about anything I can think of. Leadership requires making tough decisions to go on when everyone wants to quit. We have been there countless times.

As a leader, you know that the destination is just ahead and you are determined to get everyone there.

One such person, who was determined to reach his destination no matter the circumstances, was the Apostle Paul. A story in Acts chapter 27 reflects just how true this is. Paul was a prisoner and had he not appealed to Caesar, he might have been set free; but he had a destination from God to reach kings, so he could not settle for anything less. There he was, a prisoner on board a ship trying to make it to Rome in the height of storm season. Instead of just being along for the ride, like every other prisoner, Paul tells the captain and crew how to do their job. He warns them not to launch out, as it would result in much damage and danger, . . . but they went anyway.

It turned out that Paul was right. After not seeing the sun or stars for many days, the ship and its passengers were in deep desperation. Paul kept his cool and encouraged the men to eat and lighten the load. He also went on to comfort them by saying an angel told him that no one would die, but that they would be shipwrecked on an island. In essence, Paul's commitment to reaching his destination saved everyone's life. His leadership got everyone to the island of Malta safely, just like he had said.

You could call Paul the "prisoner in charge." Paul provided leadership when no one else could, and he even had the privilege of getting the king of Malta healed. That was the King's anointing working through him wherever he went.

When the stars cannot be seen and all hope is lost, leaders stand up and give direction that nobody else can see. It's that kind of leadership that will open the door for a Last Day's revival of trailblazers, pathfinders, and extreme navigators who can find their way in any condition. When the disciples asked Jesus what the plan was for the restoration of the Kingdom, He told them to go into the entire world and preach the Gospel. The plan was *them;* the plan was *leadership.*

This book is designed to help leaders like you look up, see the light, and find their "**N**," so you can steer your team in the right direction. I've taken words that begin with the "**N**" sound and attached leadership principles and experiences to them, in order to help you get perspective on where you are and where you need to go. It's important to have and adhere to instructions from above in order to take those following you to a place of fulfillment and fruitfulness. When you are gone, there will be leaders who continue to carry on the mission. That was Jesus' leadership example.

As a leader, I want you to be **N-SPIRED**, **N-ERGIZED**, and **N-COURAGED** for the adventure that is ahead of you. I pray that you will **N-JOY** navigating your team to the new world.

Let the adventure begin!

N-ABLE

|en·able|

[to provide with the means or opportunity]
[to give legal power, capacity, or sanction to]

Jesus N-ABLED twelve men to change the world. Who are you N-ABLING to make a difference in your world?

When you **N-ABLE** someone, you give them the power and the authority to do what needs to be accomplished in a situation. We have noticed something about our two grown sons when they come home for a visit. Without question or hesitation, they make their way to the refrigerator to see what snacks or drinks are available. (Some things never change, even with age!) Why do they have this freedom? It's simple. They are home, and they are our sons . . . not strangers. If they were visitors, they would not even consider checking out the refrigerator because that would be rude and overstepping their boundaries. But our children have been **N-ABLED**, and they have the authority, the knowledge, and the ability to go and help themselves in our home. (Now, our grandkids help themselves to the refrigerator, too.) You see, it is part of their inheritance. Most of all, they know they are at home, and they have access to whatever they want.

We are God's sons and daughters, and He has **N-ABLED** us and given us the authority and power to accomplish what needs to be done in any situation. God makes it possible for us to be a blessing in any situation to other people.

> *"When Apollos wanted to travel to Greece, the believers in Ephesus encouraged him. They wrote to the disciples in Greece to tell them to welcome him. When he arrived in Greece, God's kindness ENABLED him to help the believers a great deal."*
>
> **Acts 18:27 (GW)**

Have you ever wanted to help or **N-ABLE** someone? Here, in Acts chapter 18, the believers in Ephesus wrote to the disciples in Greece and encouraged them to welcome Apollos when he came. When you put in a good word for someone, you are backing them up. You are, in essence, giving your approval and blessing to that person; so whoever you have favor with, they also will find favor. They can walk freely because your relationship with others has paved the way for them to stand in your authority. Their gift is received because you have **N-ABLED** them to walk in your favor.

What door of favor can you open this week for someone by using your influence to N-ABLE them?

N-COURAGE

| en·cour·age |

[to inspire with courage, spirit, or hope]
[to spur on]
[to give help or patronage to]

When you N-COURAGE someone, you give them the gift of believing in themselves. Have you N-COURAGED someone today?

After we graduated from Christ for the Nations Institute, we took our very first full-time youth pastor's job with a church in Dallas which ran about 50 people. In the beginning, we literally (and physically) had to build our own Sunday school rooms. During the time we were there, the church grew to over 8,000 people with a satellite network of over 1,000 churches across the United States. We had the opportunity to do things that most youth pastors only dream about. Things like producing a children's television program, which broadcast for three years around the world, and creating a national youth convention called *Youth WAVE*, which drew over 2,500 teenagers and leaders each year. We produced concerts with the day's top Christian music artists, including Russ Taff, Whiteheart, Phil Keaggy, Mylon Le Fevre, DeGarmo and Key, and others. Why were we able to do all these things and more? Because we had a pastor who believed in us and the calling of God on our lives. He met with us every quarter and **N-COURAGED** us in what we were doing. He gave us the freedom to run with the vision, which gave us the courage we needed to dream big and do more for God.

> *"ENCOURAGE young men to use good judgment."*
>
> **Titus 2:6 (GW)**

Timothy was probably in his early 30's when he started pastoring the church at Ephesus, which became the largest Christian congregation of his time. Among his members were believed to have been Mary, the mother of Jesus; and the Apostle John, after he returned from the Isle of Patmos with the "Revelation." That would be intimidating enough, but the Apostle Paul had trained Timothy and continued to speak into him strength, wisdom, and courage through his letters. In one such letter, he **N-COURAGED** Timothy to not even consider his age to be a hindrance, but to teach those older the truth of God's Word. (1 Timothy 4:12)

The **N-COURAGEMENT** that Paul gave to young Timothy translated into leadership that rocked his generation and provided a model for discipleship which we can still use today.

Who do you know that you can N-COURAGE today?

N-CIRCLE

| en·cir·cle |

[to form a circle around]
[to pass completely around]
[to surround]

N-CIRCLE yourself with people who build your faith. Who can you N-CIRCLE and surround yourself with that stirs your soul to great faith?

I love Europe and have had a heart for the Europeans for many years. Not only do I love the food and the culture, but I love the churches and ministries God has placed there. My friend, Mal Fletcher, founded Youth Alive in Australia, and then God called he and his wife, Davina, to move to Europe. For their first 10 years, they based in Copenhagen and then relocated to London, where Mal is a media commentator, broadcaster, and business leadership consultant. For several years, I had the privilege of attending a by-invitation-only conference hosted by Mal that is a think-tank forum. What I learned more than anything in those meetings was this: If you do not want to get sterile or caught up in a religious rut, **N-CIRCLE** yourself with people who challenge your thinking. Like Mal says, "Influence your world more than it influences you. Make God Famous!"

"There came Jews from Antioch and Iconium and having persuaded the crowds stoned Paul, drew him out of the city, supposing him to have died. But while the disciples ENCIRCLED him, he rose up and entered into the city. And on the morrow he went away with Barnabas to Derbe."

Acts 14:19-20 (Darby)

There's something very powerful about gathering together with friends who understand what you have been through or have experienced a level in God that you desire, and they know how to pray. When people you respect **N-CIRCLE** you, it causes your faith to rise, helping you believe that anything is possible. They **N-CIRCLE** you and impart strength, so you can get up and take hold of the direction God has given you and face whatever gets in your way with unflinching confidence. In the Old West days, it was called circling the wagons!

Who N-CIRCLES you with faith that makes you get up and go?

N-COUNTER

| en·coun·ter |

[to come upon face-to-face]
[to come upon or experience especially unexpectedly]

Everywhere Jesus went, people's lives were changed forever. When you N-COUNTER Him, it leaves a permanent mark on your soul.

My first year at Bible college, I shared a three-bedroom, two and one-half bath apartment with 15 other guys. That's right, 15. One rare Saturday morning, everyone was gone but me. I emptied the closet for added privacy and gave the whole day to God, just to tell Him how grateful I was for His love and kindness. I'm not sure how much time had passed, but it was as if God had opened the top of that closet and climbed in there with me. It was so overwhelming that I began to shake. The intensity of His presence kept growing until I thought I would explode. Literally, I had to ask Him to stop, because I just could not take anymore. That one **N-COUNTER** changed my life forever and made me hungry for more of Him!

> *"John told them, 'I baptize with water, but right here in the crowd is someone you do not recognize'. . . . This ENCOUNTER took place in Bethany, an area east of the Jordan River, where John was baptizing!"*

John 1:26, 28 (NLT)

Jesus spent 30 years being a son, a brother, a carpenter, and a friend to those He knew in His hometown of Nazareth. His ministry was not launched until John baptized Him in the Jordan River and the Holy Spirit was released to reveal, to everyone's surprise, who He really was: the Son of the Living God.

You might be someone's surprise in much the same way. As you are walking with God and seeking His direction for your life, you may **N-COUNTER** Jesus in such a way that it gives you a new beginning, as God reveals a different aspect of His nature to you. Then, through His **N-COUNTER** with you, you will touch and **N-COUNTER** others with His revelation. God is so vast that it takes all of us to create the bigger picture of who He is.

Put on your schedule to spend a whole morning, day, or weekend with God. Have a God N-COUNTER!

N-DEAVOR

| en·deav·or |

[to strive to achieve or reach]
[to work with set purpose]

Life is meant to be lived. What impossible task can you take on as a faith N-DEAVOR?

I n 1996, we were in Brisbane, Australia conducting the youth meetings for Kenneth Copeland's Believers' Convention, when the Lord spoke to my heart and said, **"Go back to the Dallas/Fort Worth area and start a youth church. Father the fatherless and show them My love!"** At the time, this concept was practically unheard of. To launch a ministry to hurting young people with little opportunity for financial support seemed like an impossible endeavor. So, we did it. Why not, right? If God said to do it, then it's up to Him to provide. Support came from here and there, and lives were changed. We had weekly worship, concerts, and started several campus fellowships. It was 10 years filled with lots of testimonies of God touching and shaping hearts and destinies, and yet so many people didn't think it was possible. It was a faith **N-DEAVOR** that we will never forget!

"Never lag in zeal and in earnest EN-DEAVOR; be aglow and burning with the Spirit, serving the Lord."

Romans 12:11 (AMP)

Paul was a fireball. Before his conversion to Christ, you couldn't stop him from persecuting the Church and throwing believers in prison. God looked down from Heaven and said, "I want Him on My team!" So, He sent Jesus to recruit him on the road to Damascus. Once Paul switched teams, he exhibited the same fiery zeal by preaching the Gospel everywhere he went, making converts and planting churches. It was only after He was imprisoned that he took this supernatural energy and put it on paper, so that generations to come could be ignited with the same holy zeal. From one **N-DEAVOR** to another, Paul gave his all. *Let's be like Paul!*

Make a list of your impossibility N-DEAVOR to-do list. Then do it!

N-DOWMENT

| en·dow·ment |

[bestowed capacity, power, or ability]

Jesus gave His disciples the power to do what He did. What gifts do you have to N-DOW to someone else?

I started playing guitar at the age of 13. I enjoyed it so much, that it quickly turned into a passion. During high school, I was in a couple of rock bands, and then in Bible College some friends and I started a drama/music group called "Glory Company" that toured the country. Later, when God called us to pastor children and youth, my passion sure came in handy for leading praise and worship; but it became much more than that. It seemed like everywhere God sent us, we naturally attracted musicians and sparked a passion for music in others. We started so many youth bands from young people who had no experience. In essence, God allowed us to **N-DOW** them with the opportunity to develop their musical gifts. Many of them became amazing worshipers and encouraged others to want to play an instrument for the glory of God!

"As each of you has received a gift (a particular spiritual talent, a gracious divine ENDOWMENT), employ it for one another as [befits] good trustees of God's many-sided grace [faithful stewards of the extremely diverse powers and gifts granted to Christians by unmerited favor]."

1 Peter 4:10 (AMP)

The Apostle Peter knew how to **N-DOW**. Jesus had given him the task of pastoring the First Church, so everything he had learned as a disciple became an experience he could pass on in training his team. His pastoral gift created pastors who raised up more pastors, who raised up more pastors, etcetera.

Your hidden abilities rise to the surface when you are around people who are gifted with the same abilities. It's like the sun coming out after a long winter. It causes the seeds to grow upwards towards the light, so they can create fruit for all to enjoy. When your gifts are developed, you possess the ability in that realm to influence others and **N-DOW** them with the power to be a blessing to the world.

How can you take what you have and N-DOW someone with it today?

N-DURANCE

| en·dur·ance |

[the ability to withstand hardship or adversity]
[the ability to sustain a prolonged stressful effort]

**The answer to your most difficult challenge is just ahead.
Your N-DURANCE will bring you to the goal. Shout: "I
CAN DO THIS!"**

I t was easy to stay in shape when I was in high school,
thanks mostly to my swimming coach. He told us that
if we ever stopped in the middle of a race because of a
cramp, swallowing water—or whatever—he would jump in
and drown us! What a nice guy, right? In other words, we
could not give up, no matter what. Having someone in your
life who expects your best effort and pushes you to your
potential is a harshly tremendous blessing. They see something in you and drive you until all that is worthwhile comes
to the surface. That kind of discipline and training gives you
the strength to know how to possess the **N-DURANCE** to
keep going and the confidence to win.

"ENDURANCE creates character, and character creates confidence."

Romans 5:4 (GW)

The believers in the Early Church had to have character and exercise **N-DURANCE** because there was no plan "B." They were it! Their lives reflected that strength in how they lived. Their giving proved their commitment to it; and they prayed like the whole world would be lost, unless they rose up and lived like real believers. We still have a lot to learn from them. Stop spoiling yourself! You are amazing, and you have tremendous abilities in you that have not been realized yet. The truth is, they never will be discovered until you push yourself to the limit with **N-DURANCE**. Exercise your brain. Train your emotions. Push yourself to do more. Grow and achieve until nothing and no one can stop you from being at the top of your game. *Learn from the best and help all the rest.* God created you for greatness. Believe it!

Picture yourself with ultimate N-DURANCE, planting your flag at the top of your Mount Everest and reaching your goals!

N-ERGIZE

| en·er·gize |

[to make energetic, vigorous, or active]
[to impart energy to]
[to apply voltage to]

You activate your faith by believing in your heart and declaring with your mouth. Open both and N-ERGIZE your life.

Have you ever gotten a new bank card in the mail but couldn't use it immediately? Sure, we all have. Before you can start using it, you have to call and answer a series of qualifying questions, which puts a number of safety measures in place. This secures your bank information and protects it from intruders. Once this is completed, you can activate your card and money can come and go at your command. The account is **N-ERGIZED**, so that you have buying power! How interesting that the only way to activate your card is by talking into an automated program and speaking the right words. Nothing is available to you until you speak something into the phone.

Life operates on that same principle.

"For [if we are] in Christ Jesus, neither circumcision nor uncircumcision counts for anything, but only faith activated and ENERGIZED and expressed and working through love."

Galatians 5:6 (AMP)

When your heart is full of faith in God's love, then your words become containers which carry that love to everyone you speak to. Your inspiring words will create smiles, favor, and open doors because people perceive in you a genuine heart that wants to bless them; and they respond accordingly. No matter how difficult the situation may seem, your words can be disarming and cause people to take down their emotional defenses and open up to the blessing that you are. People's hearts—much like your new bank card—are voice-activated and **N-ERGIZED** by your positive believing and speaking. When you do it right, you can open every door along the way.

Whose faith can you activate today with words that N-ERGIZE?

N-FORCE

| en·force |

[to give force to]
[to urge with energy]

N-FORCE who you are. Tell the devil to shut up and believe in who God has created you to be!

I n 1984, President Ronald Reagan signed the Equal Access Act, enabling students to start and run a Bible study on their public school campus. It was an amazing opportunity. We immediately began leadership training for teens to go into their schools and make a difference. One young man approached his high school principal and asked permission to start a Bible study, and the principal responded, "No, absolutely not." The young man asked for a reason and the principal said, "Because of separation of Church and mind!" That was one of the funniest responses I had ever heard. Armed with a copy of the Equal Access Act, the teen returned and **N-FORCED** his rights to start a meeting . . . and he did . . . reaching out to other students on his campus.

"From the time of John the Baptizer until now, the kingdom of heaven has been forcefully advancing, and forceful people have been ENFORCING it."

Matthew 11:12 (Paraphrased)

Jesus knew who He was and **N-FORCED** it. He preached about who He was in Luke 4:18 and then proved it with miracles, signs, and wonders. Take ownership of who God says you are and put a demand on Heaven to back you up. A policeman doesn't make the laws, but he **N-FORCES** them with his granted authority. Be more aggressive about **N-FORCING** the reality of who you are. If you stand up and possess the supernatural promises of God, you will see God-sized results!

What has God shown you about your calling that you need to N-FORCE?

N-GAGE

| en·gage |

[to bind (as oneself) to do something]
[to bind by a pledge to marry]

Don't hide from your destiny. N-GAGE your calling and step into your future. Tell God, "Here I am!"

While teaching a third-year youth ministry class at Christ for the Nations Institute, one of the students shared their recent engagement story with the class. It quickly became the topic of that entire session, as one-by-one each student shared their amazing engagement adventures. One young man arranged for the movie theater to pop the question, fully personalized on the big screen before the movie. Another was at a baseball game and the whole ballpark got to be in on it via video. My favorite was one young man who was taking his girlfriend on a date on his motorcycle and pretended to run out of gas. As they walked along, they passed some buildings and a massive billboard became visible that said, "Will you marry me?" All happy endings. But the most impressive thing to me was the giant effort these brave souls made to **N-GAGE** their future mate.

> *"'I will cause him to draw near, and he shall approach unto me; for who is this that ENGAGED His heart to approach unto me?' saith the Lord. 'And ye shall be my people and I will be your God.'"*

Jeremiah 30:21b-22 (KJV)

God is all about relationship and has an amazing destiny in store for you; but the only way to experience it is by connecting to Him. If you could do it all on your own without a deeply personal, constant dependence on Him, then none of this would mean anything. He knows what you are going to ask before you ask it, but He wants to hear *your* voice, touch *your* heart, and then answer *your* prayer. God went to great lengths to **N-GAGE** you in salvation through His Son, Jesus. He came into your heart; now the question is, will you come into His?

What can you do today to N-GAGE your destiny?

N-GULFED

| en·gulf·ed |

[flowing over and enclosed]

God is vast. His love for you is larger than the universe. When is the last time you allowed God to N-GULF you?

A fter I finished ministering at a young adults meeting in Toronto, Canada, the worship team began fervently singing the song, "Your Love is Extravagant." The Spirit of God filled that place and all of us were **N-GULFED** in His presence. The power of His love began delivering people from hurts and bondages of the past. After praying for many people, I went to the back of the auditorium to get out of the way and allow God to finish the work that He had started. I will never forget that night and the way God touched and moved on His people, pouring out His extravagant love on us. To this day, whenever I hear that song, the intensity of that experience rises up in me again.

"There the angel of the Lord appeared to him in a blazing fire from the middle of a bush. Moses stared in amazement. Though the bush was ENGULFED in flames, it didn't burn up."

Exodus 3:2 (NLT)

Moses received His calling from a fire that **N-GULFED** a bush without destroying it. It is God's fire that calls you, **N-GULFS** you, and changes you into what He envisions for your life. Moses didn't think He could do what God was asking, but the presence of God **N-GULFED** him when He stood in front of Pharaoh and released words that had fire in them. The same is true for you. Your words will release whatever is burning in you. **N-GULF** yourself with God's ability, and go change your world!

Today, spend some time in the presence of God until you are N-GULFED in Him.

N-HANCE

| en·hance |

[to increase or improve in value, quality, desirability, or attractiveness]

You should be working towards constant improvement. What is undeveloped within you that you could N-HANCE today?

When God put it in my heart about writing, it was a real stretch for me. My comfort zone has always been speaking in front of people, using words to create images in people's hearts and minds that would stimulate faith and positive actions. In the past, I had tried writing but trying to form sentences in a way that made sense was very frustrating. Rarely, was I happy with anything I wrote. Then, God gave me an idea to start posting a short devotional-like blog on my Facebook® page. Each devotional was based on our *God's Ways for 30 Days!* scriptures we were sending out to our partners and friends each month. For three years, I wrote every day. And that's what I needed to do to **N-HANCE** the gift that God has given me!

"O you afflicted (city), storm-tossed and not comforted, behold, I will set your stones in fair colors (in antimony to ENHANCE their brilliance) and lay your foundations with sapphires."

Isaiah 54:11 (AMP)

The gold and jewels of heavenly gifts are inside you like an un-mined mountain. God put them there. But it will take much effort and discipline to dig them out and make them valuable. God will help you, but you need to help God. No one can steer a parked car. You have to get moving, so God can direct you! If you are a writer, you need to study writers. If you are a musician, you need to hang around musicians. If you want to be a great pastor, then you need to go spend some time with a great pastor. Find ways to **N-HANCE** the gifts God has so graciously placed within your life.

What has been lying dormant in you that needs to be N-HANCED? Today, put on your calendar to do something to N-HANCE where you want to go with God.

N-JOY

| en·joy |

[to have a good time]
[to have for one's use, benefit, or lot]
[to take pleasure or satisfaction in]

Joy is life-giving. If you deliberately N-JOY the life that God has given you, everyone else will N-JOY you more!

While on a mission trip to Mexico, we visited a small shrimping village on the gulf coast. The people there were so sweet to invite us into their homes, which were no more than shacks with shower curtains for front doors. One of our team members had bought a very expensive pair of basketball shoes for the trip and while traveling to this village, he walked through some oil that had washed ashore on the beach. It looked as though his brand new shoes were ruined, and he was very upset. This was until he met some of the village children who never even owned a pair of shoes in their life! Needless to say, his perspective changed after that encounter, and he decided to **N-JOY** the experience instead of being so upset about a pair of shoes.

"Blessed and fortunate and happy and spiritually prosperous (in that state in which the born-again child of God ENJOYS His favor and salvation) are those who hunger and thirst for righteousness (uprightness and right standing with God), for they shall be completely satisfied."

Matthew 5:6 (AMP)

It's easy to focus on what you don't have and let it make you cranky, until you see someone who has less than you do. Suddenly, you become grateful for things like sight, health, shelter, clothes, food, salvation, family, and love. At any given point in time, you realize that you have a lot more than someone else. So, **N-JOY** what God has already blessed you with, knowing He has more in store!

Make a list of 15 things that you N-JOY, then share that with your team today.

N-LARGE

| en·large |

[to make larger]
[to give greater scope to]
[to set free (as a captive)]

Jesus told the disciples, "Follow Me and I will make you fishers of men!" (Matthew 4:19) Previously, they had only caught fish. It was time to N-LARGE their pond!

One of my greatest desires in high school was to play the guitar. I also wanted to attend art school and learn marketing design. All of this was what I thought would be my future, my income, my dreams, and my direction . . . that was until God interrupted my life. It seemed like everyone who was around me continually talked about Jesus, so I decided to attend Bible College. The funny thing is, I didn't even get saved until I had moved and enrolled in school! When I started following Jesus, everything I wanted to do in high school—play guitar, design, and create things—all happened in a greater capacity than I could have ever dreamed of. Plus, they were all for a much larger purpose.

"Thou hast ENLARGED my steps under me; so that my feet did not slip."

2 Samuel 22:37 (KJV)

Whatever dreams and abilities you possess can become world-changing tools in the hands of Jesus. The Apostle Peter had a big mouth, which he always seemed to have his big foot in. But on the Day of Pentecost, the Holy Spirit took that big mouth and used it to bring 3,000 people into the Kingdom in a moment of time. If you have been having "I" problems because your whole focus has been inward, get on a bigger path where Jesus is walking and **N-LARGE** your vision.

What ability do you have that Jesus could turn into a world-changing tool? Do an intensive study on ways to N-LARGE that desire in your life.

N-LIGHTENMENT

| en·light·en·ment |

[the act or means of enlightening]
[the state of being enlightened]

**God is not hiding things. He loves to N-LIGHTEN!
What will you ask Him about today?**

I n 1978, we were living in Tyler, Texas, and experiencing
major car problems. Someone totaled our car at an
intersection, so we used the insurance money to buy an
old station wagon from a friend. Then, that car was totaled
by a drunk driver while it was parked in front of our house.
So, we borrowed our pastor's car, only to have it rear-ended
by a teenage driver on an icy patch of road. We tried to buy
a new car, but didn't have what we needed to pull it off. In
prayer one day, I specifically asked God, "What is going on
with our vehicle issues?" This is what I heard in my heart,
"When your dad was born, his dad had car trouble; and
when you were born, your dad had car trouble." Immediately,
I prayed and bound the curse of car trouble. Within 24-hours,
the dealership called and said they had just received a car
that they didn't even order! It was *exactly* the vehicle we

had asked them about, so we bought it. God had given us **N-LIGHTENMENT** about our situation, and it resulted in a transportation breakthrough!

> *"In Him all the treasures of [divine] wisdom (comprehensive insight into the ways and purposes of God) and [all the riches of spiritual] knowledge and ENLIGHTEN-MENT are stored up and lie hidden."*
>
> **Colossians 2:3 (AMP)**

Jesus knew who would betray Him, who would deny Him, who would stick with Him, and who would do anything for Him. He talked about all those things before they ever happened. He knows everything! So, if you need **N-LIGHTENMENT** about something, just ask Him. In Him is all the wisdom, knowledge, and discernment you need for any and every situation.

Write down two things that you need to know and then go find scripture verses related to them. Ask God to give you N-LIGHTENMENT that will give you the answers you desire.

N-LIST

| en·list |

[to secure the support and aid of]
[employ in advancing an interest]

You should be growing and learning every day. Better yet, N-LIST someone to grow with you. Who will you choose?

We heard about a unique ministry group that went into churches and signed up people who were interested in playing a part in a live-action presentation. The presentation was designed to draw people from the community and give them the opportunity to make a decision for Christ. One pastor who hosted this ministry group commented on how surprised he was at who signed up. It was mostly people who had never committed to do anything in the church! Once the presentation was over, the volunteers were done. The lesson the pastor learned was to provide short-term project opportunities and **N-LIST** those who have short-term commitment schedules. This way, more people would get involved!

"I urge you to pay all deference to such leaders and to ENLIST under them and be subject to them, as well as to everyone who joins and cooperates [with you] and labors earnestly."

1 Corinthians 16:16 (AMP)

Jesus experienced multiple levels of commitment from those who followed Him, and that was okay. John was the only disciple with Him at the cross along with Jesus' mother, Mary. Add Peter and James, and they made up the three closest to him. Then you had the 12 disciples, then 70 more, and the 120 intercessors in the Upper Room, all of which were directly involved in birthing the Early Church. Jesus **N-LISTED** people to learn from His anointing. You have something to offer, whether a skill, an experience, or maybe even just teaching someone else what NOT to do. God will use you to be a blessing to someone who needs what you have, but you have to look for mentoring opportunities and be pro-active.

Make a list of what unique abilities you could offer as training and N-LIST someone who can learn from your experiences.

N-RAPTURE

| en·rap·ture |

[to fill with delight]

God wants to N-RAPTURE you with His goodness. When someone captivates you to this degree, it is all you can think and talk about.

When I entered Bible College in 1974, it seemed like almost every girl there had fled from a former boyfriend and had determined to serve God and not man. For the longest time, it felt like I was in a convent. Then one day, I saw her. Blonde hair, Cancun blue eyes, and an intoxicating, joyful presence about her that was irresistible. I had almost given up; but when I saw her, I felt like it was a God-thing. Our Valentine's banquet was approaching, so I asked her, "Has anyone asked you to the banquet yet?" She said, "Yes, several guys have." "Would you go with me?" I nervously asked. When she said, "YES," my whole world changed. A year and a half later, we were married. She has been my whole life since, as we have followed God on an amazing adventure together. I was—and still am—**N-RAPTURED**!

"You have made known to me the ways of life; "You will ENRAPTURE me [diffusing my soul with joy] with and in Your presence."

Acts 2:28 (AMP)

God wants to affect you in such a way that He is ALL you can talk about. He wants to completely **N-RAPTURE** you in His love and His goodness to the degree that it changes your whole life. He gave you His all, and He still gets excited when someone like King David will let go and praise Him with all of their heart. I love Acts 2:28, which says that God has made known to us the ways of life. Some translations say the *"paths of life!"* God has a path for you, and it is solid and secure. It is full of His blessings and goodness. As you come out of self-consciousness, your soul is filled with His joy until you are **N-RAPTURED** in His presence!

Tell 10 people today about something amazing God has done to N-RAPTURE you.

N-RICH

| en·rich |

[to make rich or richer especially by the addition or increase of some desirable quality, attribute, or ingredient]

If you live in the United States, you are rich compared to most of the world. What can you do to N-RICH someone today?

When Cyndy and I got married in 1976, we didn't have a car. (We even borrowed a vehicle for our honeymoon!) Being at Bible College without a car created a desire in our hearts to help others. Years later, a young couple we knew were about to graduate from Christ for the Nations, and they didn't have a car. We went and visited them and had a wonderful time talking about vision and God's direction. Then, we surprised them by giving them one of our cars. It wasn't new or fancy, but it was sturdy and dependable . . . and FREE! They were beside themselves with joy. Thirty years later, we still remember the impact that moment had on their lives. We were so blessed to be in a position to **N-RICH** someone else!

"That I may ENRICH them that love me, and may fill their treasuries."

Proverbs 8:21 (DRA)

Never forget this thought: You have more than someone else has. Even character qualities that you learned from a teacher, a coach, or a pastor are rare commodities that need to be passed on to someone else. Meeting a physical need or just sharing a smile and a kind word that brightens someone's day could mean the world to somebody who is going through tough times. Be rich with joy, grateful for what you have, and sensitive to the needs around you, so that you can **N-RICH** the lives of those God sends your way.

Practice giving of yourself by smiling at everyone in your path today to N-RICH their day.

N-ROLLED

| en·roll·ed |

[inserted, registered, or entered into a list, catalog, or roll]
[rolled or wrapped up]
[to accept, employ, or recruit]

When Abraham believed what God said, he N-ROLLED himself into God's plan and became the "father of many nations." What are you N-ROLLED in?

As my high school graduation approached, I was struggling to figure out what to do with my life. I had started talking to God a few months earlier and was trying to understand the Bible. (Mind you, I wasn't even saved at the time!) My older brother, Steve, had invited me to visit him at Christ for the Nations Institute in Dallas, Texas. Very simply, I asked God to show me a sign. If He wanted me to go to Texas, I needed help in selling my Volkswagen. If He wanted me to stay in Michigan, I needed to get a good job. I put a "For Sale" sign on the car and it sold in just days. I had my answer. Once in Dallas, I had a job right away as a lifeguard. Steve suggested that I **N-ROLL** in summer school to make some friends which sounded like a good idea. While filling out the application, I asked Jesus into my heart. My whole life changed!

"Nevertheless, do not rejoice at this, that the spirits are subject to you, but rejoice that your names are ENROLLED in heaven."

Luke 10:20 (AMP)

God called out to Abraham, and he responded. He literally stepped right into the plan of God by deciding to walk by faith. Someone out there is waiting for you to reach out and take them by the hand, and introduce them to a brand new way of life. Their destiny might be just on the other side of an invitation from you.

Become more aware of who you can **N-ROLL** into being on your team.

List three people who you know who need encouragement to N-ROLL in a closer walk with God. Share coffee or a meal with them and help them step into their future!

N-ROUTE

| en·route |

[on or along the way]
[in transit; on the road]

When you take the responsibility of leadership, you are suddenly N-ROUTE to your destiny. Where will you go?

C yndy and I sponsored an adult ski trip for our church one winter. Our singles ministry had just gone through a horrible experience with a certain bus company, so we decided to use a different company for our trip. Come to find out, the company we found was overbooked, and they subcontracted our trip to another company—the same one our singles ministry used! We had two buses and about halfway to the ski resort, the bus in front began to blow black smoke out of its exhaust. After an awesome three days of skiing, we embarked on the return trip. Less than halfway home, the bad bus broke down! Everyone had to pack into the "good" bus. Leadership time! We instructed the driver to take us to the Amarillo airport where we flew everyone home to Dallas. That one act of leadership saved the trip, our jobs, and those people still going to the church. Some of those adults are still great friends today. **N-ROUTE** to disaster, we led the team to victory!

> *"But you will sing, sing through an all-night Holy Feast! Your hearts will burst with song, make music like the sounds of flutes on parade, ENROUTE to the mountain of God, on the way to the rock of Israel."*
>
> Isaiah 30:29 (MSG)

Whenever you are faced with big problems, face them— even if they seem overwhelming at the time. If you take charge and give it your best, it will eventually work out. If you turn and run, you cease to be **N-ROUTE** to God revealing Himself in the situation. No one said leadership was easy; but at the end of the day, you will have made an impact on those following you, and their lives will be better because of their experience **N-ROUTE!**

Identify a situation in your life that needs attention and resolve it directly and strategically. Solve the problem and open the way N-ROUTE to your destiny!

N-SURE

| en·sure |

[to secure or guarantee]
[to make safe]

Partnering with God in a leadership role N-SURES your success. Who are you leading?

I was on another trip to Mexico, this time doing a drama seminar for a church pastored by a good friend of mine. I ended up doing the training at an abandoned ranch in a sugar cane field on the side of a live volcano that continually blew smoke! "If it stops smoking, we're all in trouble," is what they told me. Just before starting to teach an evangelistic drama to the team, my brain started freaking out. As I prayed, a verse came floating up from my spirit into my heart, bringing the peace that passed all my understanding: "A good man's steps are ordered of the Lord!" (Psalms 37:23, paraphrased) I knew I was in the right place. God blessed the whole weekend, as we creatively presented the Gospel to a remote town on that smoky volcano. Many people gave their hearts to the Lord. They even asked when we could come back, which was a miracle

since this town was notoriously known for chasing missionaries out of the city limits with rocks. (Thank God I didn't
know *that* before I went!)

> *"ENSURE your servant's well-being; do
> not let the arrogant oppress me."*
>
> **Psalms 119:122 (NIV)**

God knows how to lead you, empower you, and keep
you in any situation. Keeping your spiritual ears open no
matter what's going on in your head and heart will **N-SURE**
tremendous power is available right when you need it most.
When you don't know what to do, push yourself to seek
God who **N-SURES** your victory. He will not let you down,
and your team will be amazed and trained for greatness!

**Ask God what you can do to take what you have been
given and N-SURE the growth of your team. Now do it!**

N-TER

| en·ter |

[to go or come in]
[to come or gain admission into a group]
[to make a beginning]

Leadership doors may open, but you must make the effort to walk through them. What doors of opportunity are you actively preparing to N-TER?

My first real lesson in chivalry came after I arrived at Christ for the Nations Institute. I was 17 years old with very little experience in how to be "the man." **N-TER** my brother's fiancé, Debbie. Debbie absolutely refused to get into a car until a man opened the door for her. She created leadership opportunities for us—the opportunity for us guys to step up and do what was required. We never would have thought about jumping in and driving off just for laughs; because if you knew Deb, there would be no laughing involved.

"His Lord said unto him, 'Well done, thou good and faithful servant. Thou has been faithful over a few things; I will make thee ruler over many things. ENTER thou into the joy of the Lord.'"

Matthew 25:21 (KJV)

God gives us leadership opportunities every day, but we have to open the door, **N-TER** in, and be the man or woman He has called us to be. Life is a series of choices that should culminate with us hearing Jesus say, "Well done!" Now, after years of opening the door for ladies, I can't help but think of how Debbie always expected to be treated a certain way and how the rest of us stepped up and learned to accommodate her. Thanks, Deb.

Open some doors for people to N-TER today, and make a difference by making them feel important and valuable.

N-TERPRISE

| en·ter·prise |

[a project or undertaking that is especially difficult, complicated, or risky]
[a unit of economic organization or activity; especially a business organization]

Take on leadership like a mountain waiting to be climbed. What massive N-TERPRISES are in you waiting to be developed?

We started our ministry the same year we graduated Bible college. Cyndy had taken a class on how to become a non-profit, 501(C)3 corporation, which was some of the most valuable information we could have learned at the time. Over the years, we have printed our own t-shirts, assembled our own ministry products, recorded CDs, written books and leadership manuals, all while traveling and preaching the Gospel around the world! We love travel so much that we eventually started our own travel business. I guess when God gets inside of you, it's difficult to just do one thing. We have been **N-TERPRISING** by taking opportunities that were beyond us and made them ours.

". . . the Lord preserved David in all his
ENTERPRISES, whithersoever he went."

2 Samuel 8:6 (DRA)

Here is a snapshot of David's life. His humble beginnings of worshiping God out in the field turned into a rescue mission for sheep. That turned into him being granted the opportunity to play his harp before the king. Next thing you know, David is slaying Goliath and then training a group of men in the wilderness, which eventually made him the greatest king Israel had ever known. In this entire journey, David learned how to look to God and trust Him alone in all of his **N-TERPRISES.** And, it was obvious that God was with Him. Leadership is multi-faceted and creatively expresses itself in many ways. Don't be afraid to use ALL your gifts!

**Make a list of your gifts, passions, and resources; and then
combine them into possible N-TERPRISES where God
may want to use you!**

N-THRALLED

| en·thrall·ed |

[to captivate]
[to absorb or to be gripped by]

As a leader, your presentation should captivate people's attention. What can you do to develop your speaking style so that the listeners are N-THRALLED by God's Word?

Before entering the ministry, I was involved in performing music and drama, so it was easy to incorporate those elements into our first job as youth pastors. I had a 12-string guitar that was really great, but we needed some extra punch to grab the attention of teenagers. So, I bought an electric Fender Telecaster guitar and an old Bassman amp and started using them in our youth services. The results? The youth group doubled! I quickly learned that whatever I could do to improve myself—my presentation, equipment, audio/visual appeal, etcetera—would pay off, and everyone with short attention spans would be happier!

"The king is ENTHRALLED with your beauty; honor him for he is your Lord."

Psalms 45:11 (NIV)

God is the most amazing, wonderful, loving, creative being in the universe. If you are not **N-THRALLED** by His vast goodness, then your appetites need adjusting; so you will hunger and thirst for Heaven's stuff more than the world's. As leaders, it's our job to help people focus and feed the right desires, so they can experience the **N-THRALLING** presence of our awesome God!

Watch a video of yourself giving a presentation, then develop three ways you can improve your N-THRALL factor!

N-TIRE

| en·tire |

[having no element or part left out; whole]
[complete in degree; total]
[consisting of one piece]

People believe you are genuine when you throw your N-TIRE being into your mission. What is your mission?

Social media is a generational phenomenon that has overtaken the Internet by storm. Facebook® has, at this point, surpassed Solitaire as one of the greatest time wasters ever. Even though it is an amazing tool we can all benefit from, we must be disciplined not to waste an entire day waiting to find out what our friends had for lunch. People throw their **N-TIRE** beings into some of the most mundane activities. In contrast, what if everyone on the planet simultaneously joined together online to donate, volunteer, or even move somewhere in order to eliminate hunger? Or poverty? Or human trafficking? There are many worthy causes, and so many heroes that have become the voice for these endeavors. Still, there are so many hurting people with needs. Greatness can be achieved by giving your **N-TIRE** focus to one great thing.

> *"In order that you may not grow disinter-*
> *ested and become [spiritual] sluggards, but*
> *imitators, behaving as do those who through*
> *faith (by their leaning of the ENTIRE*
> *personality on God in Christ in absolute*
> *trust and confidence in His power, wisdom,*
> *and goodness) and by practice of patient*
> *endurance and waiting are [now] inherit-*
> *ing the promises."*
>
> **Hebrews 6:12 (AMP)**

The apostle Paul had to continually help the Early Church stay focused on Jesus. So many leaders of his day were so good at being "religious." Their tendency was to take what Jesus came to do and make it about rules and regulations rather than a transformed life. Jesus came to this earth to change lives. His ministry was healing the sick, feeding the multitudes, and even raising the dead. His **N-TIRE** focus was training 12 men to do these things. Search your heart and find your mission. You may have something to share that will make a major difference in someone's life, but it only works if you throw your **N-TIRE** being into it.

Write a leadership mission statement to give your N-TIRE focus to! Read it out loud, daily. It is time to lead.

N-TRANCE

| en·trance |

[power or permission to enter; admission]
[the act of entering]
[the means or place of entry]

Open doors for others and others will open doors for you. What opportunities do you have to give N-TRANCE and promote someone else?

I n the early days of Youth WAVE Church, Christian bands were popping up all over the place. Our facilities became a concert venue for start-up groups, who would open up for better known bands, so they could get their CD's in the hands of their audience. Doing concerts was important because Internet downloads had not yet been introduced. Not only did these amazing young musicians get their start, but many also became worship leaders in other churches. We created an **N-TRANCE** for people to find Christ, discover their gifts, and grow into all they could be. Today, we are still reaping the eternal rewards.

"Wisdom takes its stand on high grounds by the wayside where the roads meet, near the gates to the city. At the ENTRANCE wisdom sings it song."

Proverbs 8:2-3 (GW)

King David introduced his son, Solomon, to kingly wisdom. In fact, much of the book of Proverbs was Godly instruction for his son, but he didn't stop there. David made sure that Solomon had all the gold, silver, and personal connections to build the house of God. Effective leadership prepares the way for greatness and then opens the doors for others to walk in. David was a *conqueror*, so that Solomon could be a *builder*. David's leadership made an **N-TRANCE** for Solomon's reign. Today, you stand on the shoulders of someone who went before you and made your place a possibility. Now, it is your turn to create an **N-TRANCE** for the next generation of leaders.

List three ways you can create an N-TRANCE for people on your team to come up to a new level in their leadership.

N-TREAT

| en·treat |

[to make an earnest request; plead]
[to plead with especially in order to persuade; ask urgently]

The passion of your N-TREATY will lead others to join your mission. What are you passionate about that you can N-TREAT others to join you?

One of our good friends, Jerry Davis, has been heading up an evangelistic disaster relief ministry for many years. When Hurricane Katrina struck the Gulf Coast, Jerry's team was one of the first to respond. Jerry and his team got the most accomplished and stayed longer than anyone else. They provided meals, clothes, support, and prayer for teams of people who came through his "Good News Tent City." During this time, we received several newsletters and updates from Jerry. His **N-TREATY** was so heartfelt, that we took our little trailer and hauled Bibles, clothes, food, and water—as much as we could afford and gather—to New Orleans over and over again. His passion became ours, because he communicated it so passionately. Not only does Jerry believe in helping people, but he **N-TREATED** others to help him fulfill it.

"I thought it necessary therefore to EN-TREAT the brothers that they would go before you and arrange the generous gift."

2 Corinthians 9:5 (WNT)

It is hard to imagine all the things Paul had to do in the First Century Church to build the Body of Christ. There were no denominations, no building programs, and the Gospel of Jesus was foreign to just about everyone. Paul knew how to make tents to support himself, but he also learned how to communicate his heart to those who believed in Jesus and moved them to join his vision of accomplishing something great. Throw yourself into your passion and don't be afraid to **N-TREAT** others to come alongside and help. If you don't have anything you are passionate about, find someone who is doing something amazing for others and passionately help them, **N-TREATING** your friends to join you.

Develop a specific tag line for the mission of your team and begin saying it, writing it, and posting it so everyone can join it. N-TREAT your team!

N-TWINE

| en·twine |

[to twine together or around]
[to embrace; knit together or weave]

Leaders must be easy to connect with. Who will you N-TWINE yourself with on the journey towards success?

We recently had the joy of welcoming our seventh grandchild into our family. With this addition, we now have three grandsons and four granddaughters. Whenever I see them, they all yell, "G-Pa!" and run and jump on me. It's nice to be so loved. Honestly, their love is fruit which has been born from the seeds of direct attention I have paid to each of them. And, it's so easy to do:

- I treat them like people and not like lesser members of society because they are children.

- I ask direct questions about their world, letting them know I am genuinely interested in their interests.

I create a true connection by engaging in conversation or play that helps them relate to me as I relate to them.

Because we are **N-TWINED** on various levels of life, they get excited about me, because they already know I am excited about them.

> *"His roots are ENTWINED . . . Behold this is the joy of his way, and out of the dust shall others grow."*
>
> **Job 8:17, 19 (Darby)**

Jesus' leadership was so connectable. When He showed up at the fishing boats, he told Peter where to fish after an unfruitful all-nighter. It took several boats to pull the catch in. That was all Peter needed to see to know that Jesus was the real deal. Jesus didn't say "Follow me and I'll make you a great religious leader!" Instead, He told Him, "I will make you fishers of men." The two were **N-TWINED** in purpose and calling from that moment. Jesus took Peter from ordinary to extraordinary simply by connecting in a relatable way.

Go out of your way to N-TWINE yourself to a member of your team today by relating to their world, even if it's something you don't know much about.

N-VELOPED

| en·vel·op·ed |

[enclosed or enfolded completely with or as if with a covering]
[to surround entirely]

Your team members need to feel safe to succeed, surrounded by your support. Can you think of a leader that N-VELOPED you with support?

When we were youth pastors, I remember one junior high retreat where we stayed up all night chasing 13 year-olds back into their dorms. Later that same weekend, we helped our church host a large event at Market Hall in downtown Dallas. After everyone was settled in and the event had begun, Cyndy and I decided to slip out and get some rest so we would be refreshed for the Sunday morning services the next day. In the parking lot, we were robbed at gunpoint. The thieves took our jewelry, keys, and wallets. Thankfully, we were unharmed but in shock at what had happened. Realizing that they had our address and the keys to our house, we feared even going home because it would not be safe. Our pastors insisted that we stay with them and sort out the rest later. They didn't have to, but they **N-VELOPED** us in the safety of their home.

"While he was still speaking, a bright cloud ENVELOPED them, and a voice from the cloud said, 'This is my son, whom I love, with him I am well pleased. Listen to Him!'"

Matthew 17:5 (NIV)

Jesus is the Good Shepherd, and He always **N-VELOPED** His team with care, love, and support. He took Peter, James, and John up to the mountain to let them experience God like He did. It changed them and prepared them for challenging times ahead. When Jesus was crucified, the Disciples were thrown into a whirlwind of emotions and spiritual uncertainty. "What do we do now? Will they kill us, too? Where do we go from here? Do we go back to fishing?" When Jesus arose from the dead, He **N-VELOPED** them with a conquering spirit. His victory over death removed their fear of death and became the launching pad for the Church to change the world.

Who on your team needs to be N-VELOPED with support and extra attention? Rally the team and do it!

N-CARNATE

| in·car·nate |

[invested with bodily and especially human nature and form]
[to be a representative]

You should be the N-CARNATION of your mission. When people meet you, are they impacted by your mission?

Not too long ago, I was showing someone a video of my grandson, Devin. They replied, "He looks just like you!" I told them that Devin looks just like his dad, Jesse, who just so happens to look like me. My younger son, Ryan, looks just like I did when I was 20, but Jesse looks like me today. I guess you could call them "generational genes," because the "Nordyke look" always shows up somewhere. Devin looks like a mini me! Does your team look like you?

"Faith in the INCARNATE Son of God; everyone who believes that Jesus is the Messiah is born of God, and everyone who loves the Father loves His child as well."

1 John 5:1 (NIV)

You are the **N-CARNATION** of the Jesus inside of you. His characteristics will come through when you seek first His Kingdom. Then, the mission that God has created you for is expressed through your life and words. If God has anointed you to be a teacher, then the words of Jesus will flow through you to instruct others. If your primary motivation is mercy, then you will be drawn to the hurting and the lonely, comforting them with the love of Jesus. You become an instrument of the Savior when you realize that what you have comes from Him and flows through you. Trees don't eat their own fruit; they produce fruit for everyone else to eat. You can always tell what type of tree it is by the fruit that hangs on its branches!

Write down what your primary passion in life is, then list three ways you can demonstrate that in a way so others can see the N-CARNATE Jesus in you. Be Jesus N-CARNATE to your team!

N-CENSE

| in·cense |

[material used to produce a fragrant odor when burned]
[a pleasing scent]
[pleasing attention]

Your passion for life should fill the room with the aroma of success. You are the N-CENSE in the atmosphere of your mission.

When we started Youth WAVE Church, everyone was amazed that an independent church just for teenagers could even make it. But, we had our own facility with monthly concerts, dinner theater events, and even started a high school that helped students who were struggling in school to graduate on time. Some students even graduated early! We were so full of vision to help young people that, wherever we went, our faith would encourage others to do things that seemed impossible. It was like opening the window on a spring day and letting all of the light and fragrance of new life into the room. We were a generational **N-CENSE!**

"The whole multitude of the people were praying outside at the hour of INCENSE! Then an angel of the Lord appeared to him, standing on the right side of the altar of INCENSE."

Luke 1:10-11 (ESV)

It had been 400 years since there was a prophet in Israel, and the elderly Zacharias took his turn doing his priestly duties at the altar of **N-CENSE**. The angel came and told him that he and his wife were going to have a baby. But instead of getting excited about the fact that they would be bringing the forerunner to the Messiah into the world, he started reasoning that they were too old. The angel literally shut Zacharias' mouth until the baby was born. Nine months later, when it was time to name the child, Zacharias suddenly blurted out, "His name is John!" Everyone was shocked and amazed and knew that God was up to something! Whatever is on the inside of you will create an atmosphere—whether faith or doubt, success or failure. Let God breathe into your soul, so that everywhere you go will become fragrant with faith; and people will open their hearts and sail into their future!

Write down three things that God has done for you recently and specifically thank God for those miracles and blessings. Then, tell at least two people a day what He has done for you. Be an N-CENSE!

N-CENTIVE

| in·cen·tive |

[something that incites a determination or action]
[a reward offered]

Total success is the reward of total commitment. What N-CENTIVE can you offer your team today?

When the church we worked for in the 1980's grew to thousands of people, we encountered three problems: (1.) We had nowhere to plug in leaders. (2.) No one knew anybody. (3.) We had very little communication concerning the needs of our congregation. The solution was to start a home group program that would answer these problems. But, who would create, implement, and maintain it? At the time, we were associate and youth pastors with all of the responsibilities of counseling, hospital visits, etcetera; plus, we hosted a weekly children's television program. One day in our weekly staff meeting, our pastor looked around the room and said, "Spencer, you can be in charge of this!" I said, "Yes, of course." We started with 70 men who hosted home groups in every area of our city. I wrote the curriculum, trained new leaders, and met with group leaders every week. My heart was to do youth ministry, but because we were totally committed to the vision of the church, God honored that by allowing us to do exactly what we had dreamed of. Eventually, we had the opportunity to host large youth conferences on satellite to thousands of teens. The **N-CENTIVE** to reach more young people kept us going!

> *"So by whatever [appeal to you there is in our mutual dwelling in Christ, by whatever] strengthening and consoling and encouraging [our relationship] in Him [affords], by whatever persuasive INCENTIVE there is in love, by whatever participation in the [Holy] Spirit [we share], and by whatever depth of affection and compassionate sympathy, fill up and complete my joy by living in harmony and being of the same mind and one in purpose."*
>
> **Philippians 2:1 (AMP)**

When you are a part of something, you need to truly be a part of it with all of your heart and not just take up space. By totally committing to the success of the team you are on, you are also committing to your own success! When facing the cross, Jesus told the Father, "Not My will, but Yours, be done." (Luke 22:42) Then He went and conquered death, hell, and the grave and paid for our salvation with His own blood. His total commitment to you should make you want to be totally committed to Him. When He wins, you win. You are on His team. That's a great **N-CENTIVE**!

Reward someone and give them an N-CENTIVE today by telling them how valuable they are to the success of the team. Give your team forward N-CENTIVES!

N-CLINE

| in·cline |

[to lean, tend, or become drawn toward an opinion or course of conduct]

"Lift up your ear to my sayings!" were King David's leadership instructions to Solomon. Get your team to N-CLINE their attention towards success.

Have you ever been somewhere and your cell phone had a tough time getting a decent signal? It's funny watching people walking around holding up their phone, trying to receive better reception, so they can finish a conversation. (It's not so funny when you are the dork doing it!) When they finally get enough bars to function, it's like they are back in control of their life again. It wasn't that long ago when every phone had a cord, and sometimes you even had to share a "party line" with someone in your neighborhood. Wow, our expectations are so much higher than they used to be! When the culture around us moves upward, we can move up, too—setting the direction of our team to receive the signal of success.

> *"That He may INCLINE our hearts to Him, to walk in all His ways and to keep His commandments, His statutes, and His precepts which He commanded our fathers."*
>
> **1 Kings 8:58 (AMP)**

Human nature tends to lead us towards living in a comfort zone; but you, as a leader, probably long for a greater adventure in life. God's ways are higher than your ways. In order to operate on His level, you have to **N-CLINE** your ears to get a clear signal; so you can hear and understand His instructions. To lead on a higher level, you need God's leadership in your life to build up your organization and team in a way that will benefit everyone. Your thoughts, words, and actions need to be on the **N-CLINE,** lifting up everyone around you. You can go higher!

Make a list of things you can do to build your team up today. N-CLINE their hearts towards success by doing something fun like taking them all to lunch!

N-CLUDE

| in·clude |

[to take in or comprise as a part of a whole or group]
[to contain between or within]

Making somebody a part of your team reinforces their value and makes them feel N-CLUDED!

When our son, Jesse, was in junior high school, he started playing the bass guitar. I remember the first time he played while I was leading praise and worship for our youth group. He was so nervous, but he did such a great job! Our younger son, Ryan, picked up playing the drums at a very young age, as well. Cyndy and I were overseeing the children's and youth meetings for Kenneth Copeland's Believers' Convention in Brisbane, Australia one year. During those meetings, Ryan was playing drums for the children's meetings, while Jesse and his friends were doing music for the teens. We were some very proud parents! By **N-CLUDING** them at a young age, they were able to grow in confidence. Both of them wound up starting several bands, recording CD's, and became awesome worship leaders themselves.

"When he comes on that day, he will receive glory from his holy people—praise from all who believe. And this INCLUDES you, for you believed what we told you about him."

2 Thessalonians 1:10 (NLT)

Jesus trained 12 men to carry on the work of the Kingdom. After He rose from the grave, He commissioned them to take His message to the whole world. He didn't come to earth to be a hero; He came to make heroes out of all of us! He **N-CLUDED** us in His mission, so that we could share the victory with Him. He could have done it all by Himself, but thank God, He **N-CLUDED** us.

Find one person on your team that you can N-CLUDE in a great way, so that you can pass on your strengths and expertise to them. N-CLUDE them in your next out of town ministry trip or special project!

N-COME

| in·come |

[a coming in]
[a gain or recurrent benefit usually measured in money
that derives from capital or labor]
[the amount of such gain received in a period of time]

Making the benefits of teamwork clearly known is almost as important as the compensation. It all adds up to N-COME!

Whenever anyone applies for a job, it is very common for them to not only ask how much it pays, but also what benefits are included. The weekly paycheck is a great thing to look forward to, but the added benefits of health insurance, transportation allowance, and employer matching for your 401(k) account make the total package so much more attractive. Our son, Ryan, worked for a time at a Children's Hospital in Dallas and one of the benefits was a rail pass for $36 for a year. That was a benefit worth knowing about. It was like getting a $1,440.00 raise in his N-COME!

"The king asked the woman about it, and she told him. Then he assigned an official to her case and said to him, 'Give back everything that belonged to her, including all the INCOME from her land from the day she left the country until now.'"

2 Kings 8:6 (NIV)

Elisha had impacted a mother's life by raising her son from the dead. This was an amazing miracle, but she was in some bad financial circumstances which caused her to lose her home and her land. While Elisha's servant was giving the king of Israel the testimony of the miracle that had taken place, this woman showed up at the palace at the same time to ask for financial help. The king immediately assigned someone to get her house and land back and all the **N-COME** from it since she lost it. In an instant, **N-COME** was created to come in!

What are three things you can do to clarify the benefits and total N-COME of being on your team?

N-COMPARABLE

| in·com·pa·ra·ble |

[eminent beyond comparison; matchless]
[not suitable for comparison]

To be an exceptional leader, you must see N-COMPARABLE excellence in others and bring it out.

There was a young man in our youth group years ago who always sat in the back, talked and goofed off most of the time, and seemed to have little interest in what we were doing at church. I played the guitar, and he was interested in learning. That later translated into him becoming part of our youth band. While we were planning a mission trip to Mexico, we put together a creative presentation to use in the churches we would visit. And guess who was right in the middle of it? The (former) back row teenager! He went from goof off to the stage and became a role model for young people in other cities. The connector? Music. Today, he is a doctor. He went from impossible to **N-COMPARABLE!**

"I tell you, among those born of women there is no one greater than John; but he that is inferior [to the other citizens] in the kingdom of God is greater [in INCOM-PARABLE privilege] than he."

Luke 7:28 (AMP)

Being an **N-COMPARABLE** leader does not mean that you are the hero, but that you become a hero maker. When you give others an opportunity to shine and you share the success and the spotlight with them, you create a legacy that lasts longer than you. John the Baptist had a mission: to introduce the world to Jesus. In response to the success of Jesus' ministry, John said, "He must increase, and I must decrease." (John 3:30) A true sign of a great leader is one who can create a platform for others to stand on and be great—even better than the leader himself.

You control the spotlight. Who can you cause to shine and become N-COMPARABLE today?

N-CORPORATE

| in·cor·po·rate |

[to unite or work into something already existent so as to
form an indistinguishable whole]
[to give material form to]

**Causing your team to blend with each other to combine
their strengths makes everyone win. Who can you
N-CORPORATE into your success?**

While on a ministry trip to New Mexico, our
group had an opportunity to experience a leadership ropes course. Each rope setting had a
specific challenge, and the team had to work together to get
through each exercise. I couldn't stand it! The instructor
made me stay off to the side with my mouth shut and not
help them strategize the solutions. I was a mess. Until then,
I never realized how ultra-parental and controlling I was.
The team did great, cruising through every obstacle, as they
wove their ideas together and built on the strengths of each
other. They **N-CORPORATED** everyone's ideas to create
solutions. I was so proud of them!

"This is what Hezekiah did throughout Judah. He did what was good and right and true to the Lord his God. Hezekiah INCORPORATED Moses' teachings and commands into worship and dedicated his life to serving God. Whatever he did for the worship in God's temple, he did whole-heartedly, and he succeeded."

2 Chronicles 31:20-21 (GW)

Having a structured environment with specific parameters is important for people to feel like there is order and that the leadership is in charge. But, within that order, there should be enough flexibility for other peoples' gifts and talents to develop and to be recognized. It's only when everyone's strengths are clearly seen that each member can take their place and contribute to the success of the whole. If individuals are stuck in positions that do not showcase their true abilities, they cannot be **N-CORPORATED** into the picture of progress that you want to create.

What amazing gifts are hidden in your team that you can N-CORPORATE this week?

N-CREASE

| in·crease |

[to become progressively greater (as in size, amount, number, or intensity)]
[to make greater; augment]

Be in a constant state of personal growth that will set the pace for the growth of your team. N-CREASE yourself!

Cyndy and I were in our twenties and associate/ youth pastors at a church that was growing so fast, we could barely keep up. Dr. John Thompson was one of our associate pastors and his wife, Susan, was the events coordinator. Susan pulled off the most amazing events we have ever seen. One time, she brought in over 1,000 pastors and their spouses from all across the United States to a conference in Marco Island, Florida. She went all out on this one and even booked a full circus with trapeze artists and rides to entertain everyone one night. Along with all the circus balloons, fireworks, and elephants, we also could indulge in all the popcorn, cotton candy, pizza, hot dogs, and ice cream that we could possibly eat. Talk about a colossal event! It just so happened that it decided to storm the night of the circus and the team had to go into full gear to move the party inside. This was just one of the fabulous things Susan pulled off. Watching and helping with all of her events taught us so much about **N-CREASING** our faith, capacity, and vision. When the opportunity came for us to do a national youth convention—which consisted of 2,500 young people in attendance, hosting special guest speakers, doing concerts at Six Flags Over Texas, renting a water park, and broadcasting to over 1,000 churches via satellite, we were able to pull it off! Why? Because we had **N-CREASED** our faith and ability to think bigger and do more.

> *"The apostles said to the Lord, 'INCREASE our faith."*
>
> **Luke 17:5 (NIV)**

Everyone in Jesus' day recognized that He had something more. Just the authority with which He spoke let them know that He had been somewhere greater, and that He could help them get to that same place. When someone knows God like that, you want to be around them; because they can increase you. You wouldn't go to a four-year-old to learn how to change the oil on your car, and you wouldn't ask an atheist how to know God better. To be a great leader, you need to constantly be learning and growing yourself, so that you can always have something to offer those you lead. Always be on the **N-CREASE!**

Find someone who is doing something you would like to know more about and schedule a meeting with them. N-CREASE your capacity!

N-DEFINITE

| in·def·i·nite |

[not definite]
[broad, inexhaustible, and unlimited]

Leadership is forever! You never stop learning, so you never stop influencing others. God's calling on your life is N-DEFINITE.

For our 30th. wedding anniversary, Cyndy and I went on a Holland America Mediterranean cruise out of Rome. Three days in the Eternal City was amazing, but the biggest surprise was visiting the island of Malta and exploring St. John's Cathedral. There, I fell in love with the stories like when 6,000 knights held off and defeated the Turkish Armada of 48,000 soldiers in a four-month battle in the summer of 1565. To actually visit and see St. John's Cathedral, where brave knights were laid to rest, and to be in that atmosphere of victory and tenacity was amazing. I still remember getting up early as we sailed into Malta and then leaving that afternoon with a whole new depth and appreciation of The Knights of St. John. The **N-DEFINITE** stand they took over and over again, defying all odds and gaining some of the greatest victories in European History, really moved me. Actually, I left there wanting to be a knight!

> *"And when they had entered [the city], they mounted [the stairs] to the upper room where they were INDEFINITELY staying—Peter and John and James and Andrew; Philip and Thomas, Bartholomew and Matthew; James son of Alphacus and Simon the Zealot, and Judas [son] of James."*
>
> **Acts 1:13 (AMP)**

Jesus told the Apostles to go to Jerusalem and wait for the Holy Spirit to come. They camped out in the Upper Room. One thing Jesus did not give them was a timeframe. So, as far as they were concerned, this is where they were to be planted for the long haul. When the Holy Spirit came on the Day of Pentecost, it changed everything; and the Early Church was born. Had they not followed Jesus' leadership instructions and committed themselves **N-DEFINITELY**, where would we be today? Once you are called as a leader, you might as well get with the program because that calling isn't going anywhere . . . but you are!

Write down what back door you need to close in order to make an N-DEFINITE commitment to your mission!

N-CESSANT

| in·ces·sant |

[continuing or following without interruption]
[unceasing]

Influence has its greatest impact through steady repetition: over and over and over again. Be N-CESSANT towards your goal!

When Cyndy and I were first talking about getting married, we discussed our feelings about being committed to each other for life and that divorce would never be an option. There was divorce in my family, and we wanted to be sure that we were on the same page concerning our future. I took Ephesians 5:22-33, Proverbs 5:15-19, and Proverbs 31:10-31, and made it a habit to pray these scriptures to lay a solid foundation for our relationship. I prayed them all the time. Not to get God to do something, but to renew my mind to the will of God concerning our lives together. We've had some rough seasons in our marriage, but we always come back stronger and more in love. I know that part of the reason is because I've prayed the will of God for our relationship **N-CESSANTLY**, until these scriptures have become a part of me. I love my wife like Christ loves the Church, because that's the way He designed it to be!

> *"For God is my witness, whom I serve with my whole spirit in preaching the gospel; how INCESSANTLY I always mention you when at my prayers!"*
>
> **Romans 1:9 (AMP)**

Paul started churches wherever he went and carried the responsibility to pray for them and be their major support system whether he was there or not. His prayers were **N-CESSANT!** If he heard that something was going wrong, he would pray until it changed. This is the kind of leadership that people are looking for. People listen to the leader who says, "We are going up! We are going to win! We are going to demolish every obstacle in our way, and we are not going to stop until we see our total success!" Be **N-CESSANT** to reach the finish line, and people will follow.

Write down three projects that need N-CESSANT action in order to see them through to completion.

N-CORRUPTIBLE

| in·cor·rupt·ible |

[incapable of corruption]
[just, loyal, moral, pure, and reliable]

One of the keys to your team's success is loyalty. When problems arise, work through them immediately. That will keep the attitude of the people N-CORRUPTIBLE!

Halfway through a ministry trip in Hollywood, California, we gathered our team together to see how everyone was holding up. We knew our team was exhausted, as we had driven straight from Dallas to Los Angeles and then hit the ground running, ministering on the streets, in a Christian night club, and in several churches. As we went around the room letting each one talk, there was one central theme: depression. Needless to say, the spiritual environment where we were was not **N-CORRUPTIBLE** and did not lend itself to joy and peace; thus, the whole team was feeling the pressure. I asked how many were dealing with negative thoughts, like suicide, and almost every leader raised their hand! Cyndy and I were shocked. As we prayed for each of our leaders, the pressure just melted away in the love and care of ministering to each other. Some wept; others joined in the praying. Something lifted off of us, and we were ready to go again. We had been corrupted by our environment and had to fix it.

> "But mostly show them all this by doing it yourself, INCORRUTIBLE in your teaching, your words solid and sane. Then anyone who is dead set against us, when he finds nothing weird or misguided, might eventually come around."
>
> **Titus 2:7-8 (MSG)**

Many times, when the Apostle Paul heard of a problem in the churches, he had to write a letter or send someone to them and try to fix it from a distance. He didn't have Skype®, he couldn't text, and he didn't have any of the modern communication methods to use that we enjoy today. Sometimes it would take months to get the message to its destination. What a privilege it is for us to be able to deal with concerns or problems quickly with a simple phone call, text, or e-mail. This type of immediate action can help solve issues before a misunderstanding turns into a major situation. Your team deserves strong leadership that will protect them from petty differences that try to come in and bring division. Your insight and determination to deal with strife will keep your teams attitude **N-CORRUPTIBLE!**

What problems exist that need your immediate attention? Go and fix it! Keep your team N-CORRUPTIBLE.

N-CREDIBLE

| in·cred·i·ble |

[too extraordinary and improbable to be believed]
[amazing; extraordinary]

If you believe you are an extraordinary leader and believe your team is amazing, they will believe it, too! You are N-CREDIBLE!

My sons grew up hearing me tell them how awesome and amazing they were and how much I loved them. This makes perfect sense because they are my sons. They helped Cyndy and I start Youth WAVE Church, so we could tell teens who didn't feel like they fit in anywhere the same thing we told our two sons: "You're awesome and amazing!" Why would we do that to strangers? Because that's what God does. The definition of **N-CREDIBLE** is something that is so extraordinary that it seems impossible. For God to think that we are so awesome and amazing is almost unbelievable; but we should believe it, because it's true!

*"See what an **INCREDIBLE** quality of love the Father has given us; that we should be permitted to be called the children of God! As so we are!"*

1 John 3:1 (AMP)

In the parable of the prodigal son, the father welcomes his son, who had blown it in every possible way, back into his family. Jesus was telling this story to God's chosen people who were the sons of the promise. They had also blown it and had violated so many opportunities that God had given them as a people, but Jesus was illustrating how the Heavenly Father was welcoming them back into His arms. God hasn't changed. We were strangers, but God came looking for us and made us His sons. That is more love than we could ever deserve, but it was His desire to choose us and call us His own. It's so extraordinary that it seems impossible, and yet it's true! Believe that you are awesome, and believe that your team is amazing. Pretty soon, they will believe it, too. Take the **N-CREDIBLE** love of the Father and do **N-CREDIBLE** things with your **N-CREDIBLE** team.

Make a list of all the N-CREDIBLE things you can think of about yourself and your team, and start sharing them.

N-DESCRIBABLE

| in·de·scrib·able |

[something that cannot be described]
[impossible; unspeakable]

Your gratitude for those who have changed your life is beyond words, and that's what you pass on to others. It's N-DESCRIBABLE!

Our first church job turned into a ten-year adventure, where we had more opportunities than anyone could deserve. At the end of it, we were so grateful. Our church had monthly satellite services and after the service was over, Cyndy and I, along with other staff members and guests, would usually go to our pastor's house for a meal. It was a great time of fellowship, discussion, and great food. We were so young and being around these amazing men and women of God was more of a blessing than we could ever imagine. We felt like kids in a candy store! It was during these times that we had the opportunity to meet people like Dr. Oral Roberts, Rex Humbard, Dr. T. L. and Daisy Osborn, Charles and Peggy Capps, Dr. Hilton Sutton, Dr. Buddy and Pat Harrison, Joe Jordan, and Dr. Norvel Hayes. What we learned about leadership, ministry, and following God was **N-DESCRIBABLE**!

"Now thanks be to God for His gift, precious beyond telling. His INDESCRIBABLE, inexpressible free gift!"

2 Corinthians 9:15 (AMP)

Jesus poured His life into 12 men who would eventually change the world. He passed on something to them that was valuable and priceless, and then believed in them to take that leadership and change the world! You have something in you that is eternally valuable, and there is someone who needs you to pour it into them. How thankful are you for the people who helped shape your faith? What you cannot put into words, you can put into actions by sharing what you have with someone else and then believing in them to go out and do the same. What will happen in people's lives will be **N-DESCRIBABLE**.

Pray and make a list of three people you can begin spending time with, so you can pass along your faith to them. The result will be N-DESCRIBABLE!

N-DESTRUCTIBLE

| in·de·struc·ti·ble |

[incapable of being destroyed, ruined, or rendered ineffective]

Leadership that is lasting is based on relationship. You cannot un-father your Dad; the link is N-DESTRUCTIBLE.

A few weeks ago, I mentioned to my dad that strep throat seemed to be going around. He asked me if I remembered the time he and I had to go to the doctor together for strep throat. I must have been only five years old. Apparently, I told him I did not want to go. He apologized and said that we had no other choice. They gave us both a massive shot that, according to Dad, "hurt like hell!" I leaned against him and cried as he held me and cried with me. Sometimes we go through painful things in life, but what makes all the difference is the fact that we have someone there who will go through it with us.

"For you are the sons of God now; the live permanent word of the living God has given you His own INDESTRUCTIBLE heredity.

1 Peter 1:23 (JBP)

Jesus, for the joy that was set before Him, endured the cross. His joy was the fact that He would soon be with the Father. The Apostles followed suit and endured painful persecution and ultimately death, because they had that same connection with the Father. They worked together and supported each other to help birth the Early Church. Once you step over the line and become born of His Spirit, that connection with God is **N-DESTRUCTIBLE**. You are His and no matter what happens, He is with you and will never leave you.

List three ways you can take an N-DESTRUCTIBLE stand with members of your team who are facing difficult situations right now. Now, go and stand with them.

121

N-DORSE

| en·dorse |

[to approve openly]
[to express support or approval of publicly and definitely]

When you have the N-DORSEMENT of someone you respect, it boosts your confidence. Who will you N-DORSE today?

Cyndy and I started attending Eagle Mountain International Church in 1988, because we heard that Kenneth Copeland was ministering at most of the Sunday morning services. At the end of the service, he would say things like, "If you think I'm going to stand at the back of the church and pat your little head on the way out, you are in the wrong church. Go out and do the Word!" That no-nonsense approach was so refreshing to us. Eventually, I was asked to preach several times when Brother Copeland was out of town. After several conversations with the convention director of Kenneth Copeland Ministries, we began organizing youth meetings for the Believer's Conventions in California, England, Australia and, of course, our hometown, Fort Worth, Texas. We still have a great relationship with the Copeland ministry to this day. Their

N-DORSEMENT of us has been a blessing in so many ways!

> *"Everyone has a good word for Demetrius—*
> *the truth itself stands up for Demetrius!*
> *We concur and you know we don't hand*
> *out ENDORSEMENTS lightly!*
>
> **3 John 1:12 (MSG)**

In this scripture, the Apostle John is giving some very personal remarks about what is happening in the Church. In the verses leading up to verse 12, He writes to the elder and prays for the church: *"Beloved, I wish above ALL things that thou mayest prosper and be in health, even as thy soul prospers."* (3 John 1:2) John goes on to talk about hospitality in the church. He also gave a warning about someone and then goes another direction and **N-DORSES** Demetrius. When you get an **N-DORSEMENT,** you have a stamp of approval on you. It's like when someone gives you a check, you **N-DORSE** the back of it. We might say you can "take it to the bank!" Just as the Apostle John did for Demetrius, as a leader, you need to **N-DORSE** those underneath you. If you are a pastor, **N-DORSE** your youth pastor. Work with those you believe in and who you can **N-DORSE.**

Today, spend some time N-DORSING two people under your leadership. Encourage them and let them know that you approve of them and will back them up.

N-FOLD

| en·fold |

[to cover with or, as if with folds, envelop]
[to clasp within the arms; embrace]

Embrace the assignment God has given you. Love your calling! N-FOLD your giftings with gratitude.

As a result of our relationship with Christian music artist, Rick Cua, I was invited to be the keynote speaker for a special Christian Family Weekend at Silver Dollar City in Branson, Missouri. Up until that time, this was the most people I had spoken to in one setting. They packed 4,000 people into the amphitheater, three times that day, for a total of 12,000 people. It was so cold that even though we had on jeans and USA leather jackets, Cyndy and I bought a blanket and wrapped it around us for most of the day. That blanket still reminds us of all the awesome relationships that God has brought to us over the years—relationships like Rick Cua.

We need to embrace the people who God has put in our lives and **N-FOLD** our calling and our friendships, as we become one and work together towards our destiny.

"And above all these put on love and ENFOLD yourselves with the bond of perfectness (which binds everything together completely in ideal harmony.)"

Colossians 3:14 (AMP)

At the Last Supper, the Apostle John leaned his head on Jesus, who was probably wearing the same seamless garment that the soldiers gambled for just a few days later at the crucifixion. John probably cringed as He watched that priceless robe fall into the hands of men who had absolutely no idea of its spiritual significance. To John, it represented the love and covering of His Master and Savior. The love and attention Jesus shared with John **N-FOLDED** him and became the theme of John's life and ministry. Everywhere he went, he was clothed with the love of Jesus!

Write down your mission and the names of those who are called to help you fulfill it and N-FOLD yourself in it every day!

N-GENDER

| en·gen·der |

[beget; procreate]
[to cause to exist or to develop; produce]
[to assume form; originate]

Do something new! It will N-GENDER faith in someone else to step out, too. What great things will you do today?

Cyndy was 8.9 months pregnant with our second son, Ryan, when God gave her the idea for us to host a youth convention at our church. We had never done anything like it before, and we didn't know anyone who had. So, we entered into absolute trust mode and forged ahead. After four years of hosting Youth With A Vision Conferences, several of our friends held similar events in different parts of the country, and youth ministry rose to a new level! We were able to use our experience to **N-GENDER** new kinds of ministry for so many churches.

"Let us all come forward and draw near with true (honest and sincere) hearts in unqualified assurance and absolute conviction ENGENDERED by faith.

Hebrews 10:22a (AMP)

Before Jesus, no one had ever walked on water. So, when He showed up in the middle of a stormy lake, the Disciples were not prepared and didn't know what to think, say, or do. They were experienced fishermen who were familiar with ships, storms, and waves; but this was "out of the boat," so to speak. Jesus said, "Don't be afraid. It's me!" Peter—quite possibly before He could think—said, "If it is you, get me to come to you on the water!" (Matthew 14:28). Jesus said, "Come," and Peter walked on water, too! Many times, you could be presented with an unfamiliar challenge or a new opportunity that you have no experience in handling gracefully. That's when you have to step into absolute trust and not think about whether it makes sense or not. The results will be exhilarating and will **N-GENDER** faith both now and in the future to all who hear about it.

What storms do you need to jump into the middle of right now to N-GENDER forward motion for your team?

N-SUE

| en·sue |

[to strive to attain; pursue]
[to take place afterward or as a result]

When you believe God can, and you can, success will
N-SUE! What will you believe for right now?

Transitions can be challenging, especially when you
are a church leader. Not only is your job affected,
but your whole way of life—financially, socially, and
spiritually—can change. When you are a leader at your home
church, it is your exclusive social and spiritual family. Every
time we left a church to take on a new assignment, the
temptation was to treat the church we were leaving and
the transition like a divorce in terms of rejection, hurt,
and separation. Each time, we determined in our hearts not
to give in to the temptation, but decided that whoever was
involved were our friends for life, and treated them as
friends instead of "ex" friends. That meant we sent them
notes, thanking them for all they did to help and bless us.
We attended meetings where they were speaking and
behaved like best friends. Every time, God's favor would

accompany us. As we pursued their success, success would **N-SUE.** We are still friends with a great number of these people today!

> *"Let him turn from evil, and do good; let him seek peace and ENSUE it."*
>
> **1 Peter 3:11 (Paraphrased)**

In 2 Kings, chapters 22 and 23, a teenage king named Josiah was brought a book and had the priest read it to him. The minute he heard the words of God, he tore his clothes and began a transition to take God's people out of the judgment zone and back into the blessing. He could have rebelled like the kings before him, or he could have fallen into despair after hearing what God was going to do to those who rejected Him. Instead, he decided to believe the best and do what was right. As a result, judgment was delayed during his life and reign. He cleaned up the kingdom by renouncing idolatry, and restoring faith in God. In a transition, if you choose to believe in success and act on it, success will **N-SUE.**

What thinking patterns need to be implemented in your team for success to N-SUE?

N-TAILS

| en·tails |

[to confer, assign, or transmit (something) for an
indefinitely long time]
[to impose, involve, or imply as a necessary accompaniment
or result]

Leadership is not a business catchphrase but a lifestyle. It
N-TAILS adjusting everything you think, feel, say, and do
in order to effectively influence your world.

We've had several homes built, and it is amazing
how many details are involved. You get to pick
out the carpet, the floors, the tile, the faucets,
the fixtures, and changes in the floor plans. It was these
specific details that made a huge difference in the look and
feel of the house. In one home we were building, a friend
suggested we wire the place with double phone and cable
connections before they put in the sheetrock, so we did. As
a result, we had phone and TV cable connections in every
room of our six-bedroom house, plus all four bathrooms.
Hello? What a difference some up-front attention made!
The same is true in life. Making your life easier to manage
will **N-TAIL** paying attention to the little things and thinking things through to the end—even from the beginning.

"Accept, as I do, all the hardship that faithfulness to the gospel ENTAILS in the strength that God gives you!"

2 Timothy 1:8 (JBP)

When God put it in Nehemiah's heart to rebuild the walls of Jerusalem, I am sure Nehemiah did not think about all the details that would be involved. He would need permission, financial backing, leadership influence, and favor with people who had no idea who he was. He went from being a cupbearer for the king of Babylon, to becoming the rebuilder of God's Kingdom. That is quite a jump in responsibility. One detail he had to deal with was the opposition to this project. Every construction worker had to also physically defend what he was building. They all had to be "Warrior Wall Builders" with a hammer in one hand and a sword in the other. When you take on a leadership role, have the foresight to examine the details of each project that is before you. Consider everything they **N-TAIL**. By doing this, you will be prepared to take your project and team to victory and save you a lot of hassle.

Write out everything your project N-TAILS and give every detail some serious thought.

N-TRUST

| en·trust |

[to confer a trust on; to deliver something in trust to]
[to commit to another with confidence]

Leaders earn the right to be followed. What will you N-TRUST to your team today?

As youth pastors and senior pastors, our major emphasis was leadership development. Our personalities have always had a tendency of doing everything ourselves; but, when it came to reaching out to high school campuses, any effort had to be student-initiated and student-led. This was the perfect opportunity to **N-TRUST** young people with leadership roles. We established Youth WAVE campus pastors who were students at the campus. Not only did they start Bible clubs and prayer meetings at their schools, many of them totally stepped out and hosted events on campus. One young lady put a Christian concert together in her school's auditorium one morning before classes started. Another young man set up a "free drinks" event on the day school let out for summer break. They had live music, passed out soft drinks and bottled waters, plus handed each student a copy of the Gospel of John that was appropriately titled *Living Water!* We **N-TRUSTED** those students with responsibility, because they proved themselves trustworthy.

> *"And the things you have heard from me among many witnesses, ENTRUST these to faithful men who will be able to teach others also."*
>
> **2 Timothy 2:2 (ESV)**

The fact that Jesus gave the entire responsibility of reaching the world with the Gospel to 11 guys—10 of which ran and hid when the going got tough—has always inspired me. Talk about trust! He saw their potential to be great, to rise up and believe, and He also must have seen their ability to **N-TRUST** that same leadership to those who would follow their example. The cool thing about it was . . . it worked. God took imperfect, unstable, unpredictable people and used them to change the world. If you think you are the only one who can get the job done, think again. Be brave enough to **N-TRUST** those under you to do great things.

Make a list of three of the most faithful people on your team and N-TRUST them with more!

N-TRENCHED

| en·trench·ed |

[to place within or surround with a trench especially for defense]
[to anchor, fortify, or strengthen your position]

The solid position you lead from will create stability in those who follow you. N-TRENCH yourself in leadership!

I showed up to Bible college as a 17 year-old kid with no direction or clue as to which way to go with my life. It did not take long for me to realize that I wasn't the only one with this dilemma, as I was surrounded by many young adults who were in the exact same state of mind. But there, we wanted more of God. The emphasis of the school was prayer, praise, and world missions. We had all-night prayer meetings and started each morning with worship. People from all over the world came to be saturated in the presence of God, so they could go back to their nations and make a difference. Every day, we were **N-TRENCHED** in a passionate desire to be changed, so that we could change our world. It defined who I am.

"Have the roots of your being firmly and deeply planted in Him, ENTRENCHED and found in Him, being continually built up in Him, becoming more confirmed and established in the faith."

Colossians 2:7 (Paraphrased)

In Acts 3:4, Peter and John went to the temple to pray and on their way inside, healed a crippled man. When this man—whom everyone knew was crippled and begged at the gate every day—began running and jumping and shouting praises to God, it gave Peter and John a marvelous opportunity to preach to the crowd who watched in amazement. Everyone was speechless, as they heard these men declare salvation through faith in Jesus. Even though they looked normal, it was obvious these two disciples prayed, preached, and healed the incurable just like Jesus did. Whatever you are **N-TRENCHED** in is what becomes obvious to others.

List three areas of your life you could adjust to be more N-TRENCHED in the leadership of Jesus!

N-DICATION

| in·di·ca·tion |

[something that serves to indicate]
[the action of indicating]
[manifestation; mark; proof of something]

You should be leaving undeniable evidence of your leadership and influence wherever you go. It's an N-DICATION that you are called to lead.

One time while ministering in northern Tennessee, I took Cyndy and our boys to the Red River Revival Grounds on the Kentucky border. For three years, several ministers gathered in this small, log-cabin-style chapel to pray, asking God to bring revival to an area that was notorious for outlaws and saloons. In the early 1800's, God answered their prayers and visited that region with one of the greatest revivals ever recorded in the United States. Thousands would come and camp out because there were no hotels, thus the term "campmeeting" was born. People would become overwhelmed by the presence of God and at one time, there would be more people attending the meetings than the entire population of Kentucky! Quickly, the saloons in nearby towns were replaced with churches and businesses. The lives of the people were changed forever. It was quite awesome to stand on the same grounds as that great revival and read the names of men and women on their tombstones who may otherwise had been forgotten, except they met the Lord there. It was an **N-DICATION** that God had changed lives and our nation.

> *"Even if others think I am not an apostle,*
> *I certainly am to you. You yourselves are*
> *the INDICATION that I am the Lord's*
> *apostle."*
>
> **1 Corinthians 9:2 (Paraphrased)**

Jesus didn't build buildings; instead, He built people. The one thing He left behind was a group of men who had been changed, transformed, and filled with His Spirit. The Lord Jesus exemplified leadership, and those who followed Him were the **N-DICATION** that everything He taught was the absolute truth. And, it continues to change hearts and lives today. The Apostle Paul came later and after his encounter with Jesus on the road to Damascus, he became a leader like Jesus. Everywhere Paul went, churches were born. The leadership anointing that was on his life raised up more leaders, and that was the **N-DICATION** of his calling!

What will you leave as an N-DICATION of your
leadership?

N-DISPENSABLE

| in·dis·pens·able |

[not subject to being set aside or neglected]
[absolutely necessary; essential]

Your leadership is necessary to this generation. Otherwise, you would have been born some other time. As far as God is concerned, you are N-DISPENSABLE.

While I was an instructor at a Bible college, another minister was teaching the students that they needed to be a "Blessing Dispenser." Several thought she was saying to be a "Blessing to Spencer" and wondered what kind of difficult situation I was going through that required everyone to be a blessing to me! When the misunderstanding was cleared up, we all had a good laugh over how easy it is to say one thing and have people hear something completely different. In their defense, one of the definitions of my name "Spencer" is: "dispenser of provisions!" God's desire is to dispense His blessings on our generation, but He needs dispensers. He won't do it by Himself; God wants to partner with us to bring His glory to all the earth. The moment we give ourselves to Him, we become **N-DISPENSABLE** to our generation.

"The eye cannot say to the hand, 'I don't need you!' and the head cannot say to the feet, 'I don't need you!' On the contrary, those parts of the body that seem to be weaker are INDISPENSABLE."

2 Corinthians 12:21-22 (NIV)

In Matthew chapter 16, Jesus asked His disciples, "Who do you say that I am?" Simon answered, "You are the Christ, the Son of the Living God." Jesus blessed him, changed his name to Peter (meaning "a piece of the rock"), and said, "Upon this rock I will build My church, and the gates of Hell will not prevail against it!" A few verses later, Peter rebukes Jesus for talking about the crucifixion to come, and Jesus had to rebuke Peter. In spite of all Peter's ups and downs, Jesus never gave up on him. He always spoke to the potential inside of Peter, knowing what greatness he was capable of. God will never give up on you, either. He looks beyond your failures and sees you as **N-DISPENSABLE**.

Think of someone on your team who needs to shake off a bad experience, and go reassure them that, to you, they are N-DISPENSABLE!

N-DISPUTABLE

| in·dis·put·able |

[not disputable]
[unquestionable]

You should be so convinced of your call to leadership that no one would dare challenge it. You have N-DISPUTABLE influence on those you lead.

B efore we had grandkids, I decided on our grandparent names because I didn't want to be called something like "Pee-Pee" or "Poo-Poo" by short people running around our house. We chose "G-Pa" and "G-ma," because it made perfect sense—G stood for "grand," and it was easy to say. Now, when my grandkids call me something like "Pee-Paw" by accident, I call them by some strange and dorky name, to which they reply, "That's not my name!" I then remind them that my name does not have any "pee" in it. What this simply means is, I know who I am—and I firmly stand on it. Just as importantly, I also know who I am *not*. I am not their parent and thus am not responsible for their discipline and major instruction in life. I am a support system to my kids and grandkids, offering encouragement and perspective when asked, but I do not make decisions for them. It works well when we stay within the framework

of our role. There, my position with its responsibilities is
N-DISPUTABLE.

> *"Then the Master, Jesus, after briefing
> them, was taken up to Heaven, and He
> sat down beside God in the place of
> honor. And the disciples went everywhere
> preaching, the Master working right with
> them, validating the message with IN-
> DISPUTABLE evidence.*

Mark 16:19-20 (MSG)

In Numbers chapter 16, God had established Moses and
Aaron as leaders; but Korah, Dathan, and Abiram were not
happy with that decision. Even though Korah was a Levite,
chosen by God to serve in the tabernacle, he didn't think it
was fair that Moses should be in charge. The whole thing
became a showdown with Moses telling everyone to get
away from these three and whoever was siding with them.
Then, the ground opened up and swallowed Korah, Dathan,
Abiram, along with their families, tents, and all their belongings. Immediately following, fire came and burned up 250
men who had fallen for Korah's rebellion. After all of this
confirmation, Moses' position was **N-DISPUTABLE.** Your
position in God is solid, and your leadership should reflect
the fact that God has put you where you are. Now, act like it.

**Write down three areas of your leadership where you can
be more proactive in making your influence
N-DISPUTABLE.**

N-CONSPICUOUS

| in·con·spic·u·ous |

[not readily noticeable]
[concealed, subtle, and unassuming]

Blowing your own horn is just noise. Being a behind-the-scenes influence produces great results. Be famous as a team and N-CONSPICUOUS as an individual.

While on staff at a large, well-known church, one of my responsibilities was hospital visitation to our members. Sometimes, it would break my heart to find out some of them were too embarrassed to call for a visit, simply because they felt their faith wasn't strong enough to get healed on their own. I would always assure them that the Gospel was all about caring and standing with each other. One woman I visited looked to be in really bad shape, but I assured her that Jesus was the Healer and laid my hands on her and prayed for healing. About six weeks later, she approached me at church and handed me a set of cuff links as a "thank you" gift. She then told me the whole story of how she had fallen down a flight of stairs, how her kidneys were failing, and that she had been bitten by a poisonous spider. The doctors had given her two weeks to live; but when I prayed for her, she got better! I am not even sure she knew my name; it was so **N-CONSPICUOUS!**

> *"Abruptly, Jesus broke into prayer: Thank You, Father, Lord of Heaven and Earth. You've concealed Your ways from sophisticates and know-it-alls, but spelled them out clearly to INCONSPICUOUS people. Yes, Father, that's the way You like to work."*

Matthew 11:25-26 (Paraphrased)

Once upon a time, there was one little maid . . . in one little Bible verse . . . who said one little thing that saved the life of an influential leader. Naaman's impressive credentials are listed in 2 Kings 5:1, but he had a major problem: He was a leper. Everyone knew leprosy was incurable; but Naaman's wife had an Israelite maid who said he could be healed if he went and found the prophet, Elisha. You can read the whole story yourself, but the end result was Naaman's total and complete healing from leprosy. It all happened because a little maid, whose name we will never know, shared her faith. Who was she? Just an **N-CONSPICUOUS** believer making a major difference.

Write down three behind-the-scenes, N-CONSPICUOUS actions you can take to build up individuals on your team!

N-COGNITO

| in·cog·ni·to |

[with one's identity concealed]
[anonymous, disguised, or unrecognized]

Leadership is not about being bossy. The greatest among you has a servant's disguise. It's power N-COGNITO.

I love reading about Warren Buffet. As one of the richest people on the planet, he is quite **N-COGNITO**. Even though he is a genius at investing, building wealth, and turning struggling businesses from disaster to profitability, he still lives in an older house that you can bet is paid for! He doesn't look nor live like a billionaire (whatever that means). Instead, he looks like the rest of us and donates millions of dollars to worthy causes which makes the world a much better place. He is a global transformer disguised as a regular human being. I love that! It challenges me to be real and encourages all of us to be our best without trying to impress everyone, which is completely overrated.

> *"In the same way, the good deeds of some people are obvious, and the good deeds done INCOGNITO will someday come to light."*

1 Timothy 5:25 (NLT)

Joseph was his dad's favorite son, and he had a loud, brightly-colored coat to prove it. His dad's love toward him was quite obvious, even to the dismay of his own brothers. Out of jealousy, these brothers sold Joseph to slave traders who took him to Egypt and sold him to Potipher. Potipher promoted Joseph until his wife accused him of sexual harassment. That landed him in prison, where he was promoted to "chief prisoner" in charge of maintaining the dungeon. Quite a journey for someone who served so well. But, the favor of being the favorite stayed with Joseph as he went from the dungeon all the way to becoming vice-president of the nation. It pays to continue to be a leader, even in the most hidden places. Joseph had the power to be persistent even when no one was looking. He was an **N-COGNITO** leader.

What good deeds can you perform this week N-COGNITO? Come up with ways to bless three people on your team today without them knowing it was you.

N-VIRONMENT

| en·vi·ron·ment |

[the circumstances, objects, or conditions by which one
is surrounded]
[your setting, situation, or status]]

Leaders create the right **N-VIRONMENT** for success.
What can you do today to charge the atmosphere with
faith?

The first facility for Youth WAVE Church that was
truly ours was on Pipeline Road—quite the appropriate street name for Youth WAVE! When we first
arrived there, the local police department had a gang unit to
deal with many of the young people in the area who had
gotten in with the wrong crowd. Immediately, we decided to
change the **N-VIRONMENT** of our area and got busy
reaching out to these same teenagers. We incorporated foos-
ball and ping pong tables, a snack bar, a skater outreach with
ramps and rails, as well as concerts once a month featuring
local Christian bands. We also spent a lot of time praying for
the youth in our area and the events we were hosting. About
one year after Youth WAVE Church opened its doors in
this location, the police department completely closed the
gang unit because it was not needed any longer! A coincidence?
I don't think so. We had changed our **N-VIRONMENT**.

"Cheerfully pleasing God is the main thing, and that's what we aim to do, regardless of our ENVIRONMENT.

2 Corinthians 5:9 (MSG)

When Paul and Silas showed up in Philippi, they met a woman named Lydia who received them into her home after her whole family was baptized. Then, they met another girl—a fortune teller—who followed them around, yelling at them. Paul got her delivered, which made her employers mad, due to the fact that she could not tell fortunes anymore. They were so angry that they had Paul and Silas beaten and thrown into prison. When these two men started singing praises to God at midnight and all the prisoners were listening, God shook the prison so that all the doors flew open and everyone's chains fell off. The prison guard was about to kill himself, but Paul and Silas ministered to him; and he and his whole family got saved. Philippi was never the same again! Even in prison, their **N-VIRONMENT** had been transformed by their praise.

**Define the N-VIRONMENT you need for success.
You and your team create it!**

N-DIVIDUAL

| in·di·vid·u·al |

[existing as a distinct entity]
[original, select, or special]

You have such a unique set of qualities. No one will ever be able to lead exactly like you do. Develop your N-DIVIDUAL gift.

Jesus' disciples were easily recognizable because they acted like Jesus. They healed the sick, raised the dead, and weren't afraid of the religious leaders . . . just like their Master. But, even though they had trained under Jesus, each one still had their distinct characteristics. Peter had a mouth. John loved everyone. Philip was an evangelist. You could see Jesus' influence on all of them. They were all just like Him, each in their own unique way. Their experience walking with Him for three and half years caused each one of them to become an anointed **N-DIVIDUAL.**

"Train up a child in the way he should go and in keeping with his INDIVIDUAL gift or bent, and when he is old he will not depart from it."

Proverbs 22:6 (AMP)

Teaching and training are so different from each other. Teaching is sharing information, whereas training involves showing someone how to actually do something. It requires a hands-on approach that makes the difference between knowing about something and actually having experience. When you train someone, they pick up distinct characteristics of how you do it, and that leaves a specific mark on the job done. When you train under someone, some of who they are is transferred to who you are, and it becomes uniquely yours. It takes all kinds of experiences to create your **N-DIVIDUAL** trademark.

Make a list of your N-DIVIDUAL gifts that make you unique. How can you improve one of them?

N-JOIN

| en·join |

[appoint, call upon, or charge]

Your connections will either strengthen you or completely drain you. Who do you N-JOIN yourself with that makes you stronger?

When Cyndy and I graduated from Bible college, we had no idea where to go or what to do. We moved to North Dallas, and I got a job repairing and renovating warehouse spaces for rent. Cyndy volunteered every day at the little church where her parents attended. After work, I would come over and help hang sheetrock and ceiling tiles for our church of about 50 people. When it was time for the church to hire someone, they hired the people who were already doing the work—us! That church grew to thousands and impacted churches all over the world. We were given the opportunity to be a part of it simply because we **N-JOINED** ourselves to the tasks at hand!

"Now we ENJOIN you, brethren, in the name of our Lord Jesus Christ that you withdraw from every brother walking disorderly and not according to the instruction which he received from us. For ye know yourselves how ye are to imitate us, because we have not walked disorderly among you."

2 Thessalonians 3:6-7 (Darby)

Where do you want to be in 10 years? What do you desire your life to look like in that same span of time? After you know the answer to these questions, the next step is to put yourself in the middle of people who are like-minded as you. Jesus chose 12 men to follow Him and be His disciples. Who did He pick from? He had many people who wanted to be with Him, to hear His words and experience God the way He did. He chose from that crowd. Are you running with the Jesus crowd or some other group? Your future depends on who you **N-JOIN** yourself to.

Today, call three people who strengthen you and N-JOIN yourself to them. Make plans to communicate to each other on a weekly basis via phone or in person.

N-TERMINGLE

| in·ter·min·gle |

[intermix]
[associate, come together, or merge]

It is only as you blend and N-TERMINGLE with others that you discover how your strengths and abilities can complement the team.

I went out for the track team in the ninth grade, and football and wrestling in tenth grade. These were good programs to be involved in, but my real sports passion was swimming. Every summer since I was eight years old, I swam on a competitive swim team and loved it! Our school finally built a pool, and we had a brand new team. When it was time to compete, I ended up swimming all of the butterfly events, because I already knew how. There was the 100-yard butterfly, the butterfly leg of the medley relay, and the individual medley that consisted of 50 yards of butterfly, backstroke, breaststroke, and freestyle. Another guy on our team, Scott, swam all the backstroke events. Together, we made a good team. We went from winning only one meet in our first year to winning over half of our meets the second year. Our coach made us N-TERMINGLE together and be a team, not a bunch of superstars. It wasn't always easy, but in the end, victory smelled really sweet to us because of all of our hard work together.

> *"God spoke to Moses: Take fragrant spices, INTERMINGLE the spices in equal proportions to make aromatic incense, holy. Now crush some of it into powder and place some of it before the testimony in the tent of meeting where I will meet with you."*

Exodus 30:34 (Paraphrased)

God had priests prepare an anointing oil that filled the temple with its unique aroma. Few things jog the memory more than the sense of smell. When the priests came out from the presence of the Lord, you knew it because you could smell them coming. Those spices coming together represented God's people **N-TERMINGLING** to become a fragrant aroma of love and unity in His Kingdom. He never forgets that smell!

How can your team N-TERMINGLE to smell like success?

N-TERMISSION

| in·ter·mis·sion |

[taking a breather, time-out, rest, or pause]
[an interval between the parts of an entertainment (as
the acts of a play)]

When you learn to stop and take a break, you will understand how to give others a break! Slow down and listen to the leadership inside you by taking an N-TERMISSION.

About once a year, I take three days and get away alone to seek God and spend an extended amount of time paying attention to Him. Those of us in Christian leadership can get so busy with the work of God that we stop flowing with the God of the work. Sometimes, we can fall into the trap of treating our Heavenly Father like Santa Claus, saying "I want one of these and one of those and some of that." You need an **N-TERMISSION** to take a break from all the noise, decisions, and situations to get away and recharge your spiritual batteries. Set aside a specific time, whether it be weekly, monthly, or yearly, to spend extended alone time with God. This will help you to be in tune with His heart and His direction for your life.

"Good friend, follow your father's good advice, don't wander off from your mother's teachings. Wrap yourself in them from head to foot; wear them like a scarf around your neck. Wherever you walk, they'll guide you; whenever you take an INTERMISSION, they'll guard you, when you wake up, they'll tell you what's next. For sound advice is a beacon, good teaching is a light, moral discipline is a life path."

Proverbs 6:20 (MSG)

Jesus often pulled away from the multitudes to spend time with His Heavenly Father. Many of these times occurred immediately after some amazing miracles. Instead of holding a press conference to advertise His awesome ministry, Jesus went away to give God the attention He deserved for all the miracles. If the Son of God made it a priority to take time to be alone with His Father, don't you think you should make time to get away and take an **N-TERMISSION** from your busy life? The results will be phenomenal.

Look at your calendar today and schedule a time of N-TERMISSION alone with God.

N-TERNAL

| in·ter·nal |

[relating or belonging to or existing within the mind]
[intrinsic; inherent]
[centralized; private; inner workings]

Building your team N-TERNALLY is more important than just having a good external image. Make sure the inner workings are working, and then you will look good on the outside, as well.

After youth pastoring for several years, I noticed that many of our quality young people—those with strong leadership skills—were moving to other churches and youth groups. This left us with lots of teens with struggles and challenges. I sought God about this, and He began to show me that I was treating our ministry like I was a fireman—running to each alarm and paying attention to every emergency. The problem with this was I spent very little time and attention developing leaders. The result was a ministry full of crisis management . . . with no leaders to help. Immediately, I began to pay more attention to those desiring involvement and responsibility. In turn, they began training leaders under them. We still helped those having emergencies, but our priorities shifted to building leaders like an architect instead of putting out fires like a fireman. It makes all the difference in the world when we strengthen the group **N-TERNALLY** by training and rewarding leadership.

> *"And the effects of righteousness will be peace (INTERNAL and external) and the result of righteousness will be quietness and confident trust forever."*
>
> **Isaiah 32:17 (AMP)**

The disciples were crossing a lake when a violent storm started to beat their ship with winds and waves so fierce, that these experienced fishermen thought they all were going to die. Jesus was sound asleep on a pillow in the middle of the storm. When Peter awoke Him, Jesus stood up and said, "Peace be still!" (Mark 4:39) After Jesus took the perfect peace that filled His heart and released it into their stormy environment, the storm immediately ceased. The lesson learned is this: If it is in you, you can use it on what's in front of you! Your **N-TERNAL** strength should be bigger than your external circumstances.

**Write down three ways you could strengthen yourself
N-TERNALLY today.**

N-TERNATIONAL

| in·ter·na·tion·al |

[of relating to, or affecting two or more nations]
[active, known, or reaching beyond national boundaries]

The world is getting smaller. Is your leadership getting larger? Your leadership could go N-TERNATIONAL!

Many years ago, I was praying for the nations, and the Lord put three specific geographical areas on my heart: Canada, Australia, and the Caribbean Islands. At first, I was somewhat puzzled because these were not areas that had intense needs like some third-world countries. So, I asked God, "What is up with that?" What came to me was that these nations were not a threat to anybody. If young people from these places were trained and equipped for ministry, they would be able to come and go fairly easily to almost any nation in the world, with little or no difficulty whatsoever. Our Father is strategic and has nations on His mind. He is an **N-TERNATIONAL** God!

> *"People from many nations will come and say, "Come let us go up to the mountain of the Lord, to the house of Jacob's God. There he will teach us his ways, and we will walk in his paths. The Lord will mediate between nations and will settle INTERNATIONAL disputes."*
>
> **Isaiah 2:3-4 (NLT)**

The Apostle Paul was limited to ministering in one place at a time, raising up leaders and planting churches . . . until he went to prison. There, he was in the position where he had to write letters to the churches in order to help train and encourage those who were being saved. What he did not realize was that those writings would become our Bible and travel across every border on the planet, spanning generations to come. God put him in the position to write, so he could reach nations and generations! He could not be everywhere at the same time, so God had him put the Gospel in print; so it could go **N-TERNATIONAL.**

Today, research a people group or a nation that is on your heart. What can you do to make a difference **N-TERNATIONALLY?**

N-TERPRET

| in·ter·pret |

[to explain or tell the meaning of]
[present in understandable terms]
[to conceive in the light of individual belief, judgment, or circumstance; construe]
[to bring to realization by performance or direction]

Learning to translate your leadership into marketable action will open worldwide doors. N-TERPRET your way into the future!

When the Lord spoke to my heart in 1996 to start a youth church—to create a safe place for them to come and worship—to father young people, I had some changing to do. What God was saying and my **N-TERPRETATION** of it, based on my own experiences in working for other churches, was quite different. One thing that helped the most was my heart for missions that was in me from the beginning of my Christian walk. I began to see these young people as their own tribe. They were a people group with a distinct culture and language who, coincidentally, did not speak "Christianese." Approaching this generational tribe in a new way was vital to being effective. We learned their culture and were very effective in reaching their generation.

"We both had dreams, they answered, but there is no one to INTERPRET them. Then Joseph said to them, 'Do not interpretations belong to God?' Tell me your dreams."

Genesis 40:8 (NIV)

When God is trying to get something across, you sometimes need an **N-TERPRETER**. Likewise, you need to know the culture and the language of your team in order to communicate effectively and move forward. Spending time working, playing, and praying together is invaluable, as you can discover the language of each team member's heart. Once you understand their heart, you know what they mean when they communicate.

What language does your team speak? Success? Momentum? Unity? Develop your team to N-TERPRET your heart.

N-TERRUPTED

| in·ter·rupt·ed |

[stopped or hindered by a breaking in]
[the breaking of uniformity or continuity of]
[to break in upon an action]

Saul became Paul because Jesus N-TERRUPTED his misguided leadership. Let Jesus N-TERRUPT you!

I n high school, I was into art and enjoyed painting and architectural design. Me and a friend created a metal sculpture for our school yard that looked like a giant arrow stuck in the ground. (It was still there, too, the last time I was in town.) I love art, especially how colors create different moods. Attending art school and studying marketing was definitely in my plans . . . until God **N-TERRUPTED** my life. What I wanted to do was based on my talents and interests, but they weren't supposed to be my focus. They were my gifts to help fulfill God's plan for my future. Today, I have the honor of using art and design in everything we do for the ministry.

"But Barnabus took him and brought him to the apostles. He told them how Saul on his journey was INTERRUPTED by the Lord and that the Lord had spoken to him, and how in Damascus he had preached fearlessly in the name of Jesus."

Acts 9:27 (Paraphrased)

Saul's training and upbringing had brought him to a place of religious fanaticism that made him want to kill anyone who was full of God. Then Saul met Jesus. He traded religion for relationship and became key in spreading the Gospel, starting churches, and authoring much of our New Testament. People can change. God may **N-TERRUPT** your plans or even lead you to help him **N-TERRUPT** someone else. Let him.

Who do you know that needs to be N-TERRUPTED? Call them!

N-TERSECTION

| in·ter·sec·tion |

[the act or process of intersecting]
[a place or area where two or more things intersect]
[the set of elements common to two or more sets]

When at the N-TERSECTION of life, God can lead you in choosing the high road—the right way and the path that will benefit the whole team. Then all YOUR dreams will come true!

Cyndy and I were walking down Bourbon Street in New Orleans, Louisiana, with our friends, Scott and Nancy Hinkle, helping with their outreach team at Mardi Gras. We brought several young people with us. In the frenzy of Fat Tuesday, we were at an **N-TERSECTION** that was packed with sinners of every kind doing what they do best . . . sinning. A young lady who was with us pushed a guy in the crowd, because he was getting real friendly with her. He came back at her like he was going to kill her. Before we knew it, the Henderson brothers, two very strong members of Scott and Nancy's team, had taken this man and physically removed him from the crowd. It's when you are in the **N-TERSECTION** of two worlds that you find out who you can trust.

"Past the first guard and then the second, they came to the iron gate that led into the city. It swung open before them on its own, and they were out on the street, free as the breeze. At the first INTER-SECTION the angel left him, going his own way. That's when Peter realized it was no dream. 'I can't believe it—this really happened! The Master sent his angel and rescued me.'"

Acts 12:10 (MSG)

Peter was fast asleep the night before his execution. Instead of cutting off somebody's ear, like He did in the Garden of Gethsemane, he let God deliver him. This time, he was letting the peace of God rule in his heart at every **N-TERSECTION**. Peter had total trust in God when he was arrested, chained, and surrounded by soldiers. During the night, an angel from God turned the lights on and struck him to wake him up, and all the doors in the prison automatically opened in front of him. Finally, in the middle of the **N-TERSECTION**, he realized God had delivered him. That's perfect peace. Let God help you at every **N-TER-SECTION**, then you can lead others with confidence and strength.

Write three decisions you need to make at the N-TERSECTION you are in right now.

N-TERSPERSE

| in·ter·sperse |

[to place something at intervals in or among]
[to diffuse or distribute within]

Persecution caused the disciples to N-TERSPERSE into all the world 10 years after Jesus told them to go. Let Jesus send you, not your circumstances.

One church we were a part of, spanning a period of 10 years, was large enough to have many pastors on staff. The core team was six associate pastors—Dr. Bill Kaiser, Bible school pastor; Mike Trent, music pastor; Stephan Steinle, children's pastor; Dr. John Thompson, senior associate pastor; Dr. Jim Adams, academy pastor; and us, as youth pastors. We all stayed at that church for a long time, and all of us are still in the ministry today! Later, after we all had grown and developed our departments, we added 10 home group pastors to help take care of the people, because we were beginning to reach our entire area. We were able to accomplish quite a bit as a team and, eventually, most of us went out and started our own churches all over the country. Our influence was multiplied and **N-TERSPERSED** throughout the world!

"Send men to INTERSPERSE and scout out the land of Canaan, which I give to the Israelites. From each tribe of their fathers you shall send a man, every one a leader among them."

Numbers 13:2 (Paraphrased)

Have you ever found yourself in a place where, in order to continue progressing, you needed to leave and plant yourself in another field? To keep leading, you must keep growing. Take your experiences in life and **N-TERSPERSE** yourself among those who have not experienced Him yet. In doing so, you can multiply your influence and get more done. If you get complacent and comfortable, you begin to get stagnant. Try something new! Go somewhere you have never been. Help someone you do not know. The whole world is waiting for you.

List three fields outside of your own where you could N-TERSPERSE your influence.

N-TERTWINE

| in·ter·twine |

[to unite by twining one with another]
[to become mutually involved]
[to braid; link; mesh together]

Jesus was eternally N-TERTWINED with His followers; but it didn't choke them, it strengthened them. Get wrapped up in your team.

One aspect of our ministry was to develop teams of young people for worship, drama, and even marketing to work our product tables. So many teenagers got experience in video production, sound engineering, and meeting/event planning that they chose those vocations after high school. Our goal wasn't activity but relationship. The experiences we had together helped shape them as people and, eventually, as leaders in the Christian community. We spent time working, praying, and playing together, and became who God wanted us to be because we were **N-TERTWINED** in purpose and passion!

"A person standing alone can be attacked and defeated, but two can stand back-to-back and conquer. Three are even better for a triple braided (INTERTWINED) cord is not easily broken."

Ecclesiastes 4:12 (NLT)

In Acts chapter four, the Early Church was experiencing tremendous birth pains through persecution from religious leaders who did not want things to change. What was their solution? They prayed and the place where they were was shaken, and they were all filled! (Notice, the *place* was shaken, not the *people*!) When you and your team come together and seek God, you all get filled and empowered to come into all that He has planned—and He has some big plans for those **N-TERTWINED** together in Him!

Take your team out and do something totally different together. You will see and understand them more than ever before as you become N-TERTWINED.

N-TERVENE

| in·ter·vene |

[to become mutually involved]
[to mix in, reconcile, or step in]

Not getting involved is not getting the job done. Most situations can be solved when true leadership N-TER-VENES.

S ometime back, we encouraged a friend of ours, who was the director of a ministry, to pastor his own church because his giftings of a shepherd were so obvious. Eventually, he took hold of this idea and went for it. Then, he did something I was not expecting—he asked us to come on board and help him! At the time, we were traveling and ministering and weren't looking for another job. Plus, we knew what it would cost us. Still, we prayed and considered what it would take to help build that church and God encouraged us to get involved. We ended up serving there three years and the church grew to three Sunday morning services. That experience was a blessing and because we were willing to change our plans and **N-TERVENE**, we saw God's blessing come in and **N-TERVENE**, as well!

"Therefore He is able also to save to the uttermost (completely, perfectly, finally, and for all time and eternity) those who come to God through Him, since He is always living to make petition to God and intercede with Him and INTERVENE for them."

Hebrews 7:25 (AMP)

I am sure Jesus was quite comfortable with the Father in Heaven, but He was the only One who could come and save Mankind. Jesus said, "Yes," and got involved in our human situation by coming into this world and taking our place on the cross. Aren't you glad He said, "Yes," to the plan of God? There are people who need your leadership. Will you say, "Yes,"? If you will **N-TERVENE** into someone else's situation, God will empower you with His ability, so that your "yes" also becomes God's "Yes!"

Write down three situations, where you need to N-TERVENE in the lives of your team!

N-TERVIEW

| in·ter·view |

[a formal consultation usually to evaluate qualifications]
[a meeting at which information obtained by a person]

You do not learn everything by asking nothing. Students of life make everyday conversations an N-TERVIEW and become wise men.

When our pastor called and told me we had six weeks to put a live children's TV program together, we knew we needed help. I immediately sought out Coach Jack Grey who hosted a TV show called, *The Bible Bowl*. These programs had the "Bible Boys" compete against the "Gospel Girls" in a Bible knowledge competition game. He was one of the nicest men I've ever met. When we first got together, he immediately asked me how many brothers and sisters Jesus had. At that time, I had no idea that Matthew 13:55 named His four brothers and the fact that He had at least two sisters! That is at least seven children, plus His mom and dad makes a family of nine. Then, Coach Jack asked me, "Imagine Jesus' whole family in a station wagon on a road trip. Doesn't that make Hebrews 4:15 come alive?" At this point, I started to wonder who was doing the **N-TERVIEWING**! Before I could even ask what Hebrews 4:15 said, he quoted it for me. "Jesus was in all points tempted as we are, yet without sin!" Right then and there, Reverend Jack Grey taught me that Bible facts are the foundations for Bible principles. I got it! I went to **N-TERVIEW** him, but that experience ended up **N-TER-VIEWING** me. That's what wise men do.

> *"After this INTERVIEW, the wise men went their way. And the star they had seen in the east guided them to Bethlehem. It went ahead of them and stopped over the place where the child was."*
>
> **Matthew 2:9 (NLT)**

The Bible doesn't say there were three wise men; it only specifies that they brought three gifts: gold, frankincense, and myrrh. There could have been 100 wise men! Have you ever noticed that even though they were considered "wise," they did not come with answers but rather questions? They had a clue about what was going on but were searching for the missing pieces, which they obtained by asking. Wise men seek out information and rely on the knowledge of others to find the truth they are looking for and go for an **N-TER-VIEW**. Only a fool thinks He knows it all!

Who can you N-TERVIEW today? Choose someone from your team to sit down with and N-TERVIEW them. Learn something about them, about life, and about success!

N-TIMACY

| in·ti·ma·cy |

[the state of being intimate]
[familiarity]
[something of personal or private nature]

Time spent in a new experience creates a closer bond between you and your team. Knowing each other's heart develops strength in N-TIMACY.

While attending a conference in Europe, one of my lifelong friends, Anthony Does, and I were invited to extend our trip and go to England for a few days. We had the privilege of visiting Steve and Charlotte Gambill, who are on staff at Life Church in Bradford, England. They were so gracious to take us into their home for a few nights, plus Steve drove us to see the home of Smith Wigglesworth and the cemetery where he is buried. This was a dream come true for me because I have always highly admired Smith Wigglesworth. His faith and miracles have always been such an inspiration to me. Today, hanging on my office wall, is a picture we took where Smith Wigglesworth preached at the Salvation Army Citadel. Every time I look at that picture, it stirs up a new **N-TIMACY** in my spirit. It also brings back the **N-TIMACY** that was created from exploring new things, being adventurous and strengthening my friendship with Anthony, plus getting to know my new friends, Steve and Charlotte. I will never forget those adventures!

> *"It is true that no one has seen God at any time. Yet the divine and only Son, who lives in the closest INTIMACY with the Father, has made him known."*
>
> **John 1:18 (JBP)**

Abraham and his son, Isaac, went up the mountain together. Joshua accompanied Moses up to Mount Sinai, where he received the Ten Commandments. Peter, James, and John went with Jesus to the mountain top and heard the voice of God. Sometimes, you need to leave your office and take your team on a trip to the mountains—or some other secluded place—and spend some time with each other and with God. On trips like these, our ministry teams would pray together, worship together, and experience life together. We always made sure to include some shopping and sightseeing time, because you can learn a lot about people when you go exploring together.

Open yourselves up to new levels of **N-TIMACY** in a new setting to get a new experience. It will strengthen your bond, and cause everyone to grow together.

Plan a getaway with your team to achieve more N-TIMACY!

N-TOXICATE

| in·tox·i·cate |

[to be drunk or ecstatic]
[to be under the influence of something]

Under the influence of the Holy Spirit, the Apostles were free from the inhibitions of their humanness. They were N-TOXICATED with supernatural freedom.

M y first trip to Australia proved to be one of the most unusual ministry experiences of my life. The youth camp where I was speaking was going along okay, but a good portion of the teens just were not connecting. One night while another young evangelist was preaching, I felt compelled to go back to my room and pray. It was the most intense intercession I have ever felt. It was as if gravity was increased 100 times over as I was stuck to the floor praying my guts out. Suddenly, I was on my feet walking like a drunk man back to the meeting hall where half of the teens were praying. I started praying for the other half. I was a crazy man, attacking anything that seemed resistant to the Holy Spirit, casting out devils, and releasing Heaven onto that unsuspecting group of kids. It seemed that everyone got set free that night. Like Peter, on the Day of Pentecost in Acts chapter two, I lost control of myself. Under the influence, God enabled me to do things I would otherwise have resisted. I was **N-TOXICATED** with God's power.

> *"These people are not INTOXICATED, as you suppose. It's only nine in the morning! No, this is what was spoken by the prophet Joel:"*
>
> **Acts 2:15 (WNT)**

When the Holy Spirit was poured out in that Upper Room, four things happened: (1.) They were all filled, (2.) they all spoke in a heavenly language, (3.) they were on fire, and (4.) they all ran out into the street and acted drunk. Everyone thought they were drunk because drunken people don't care what anyone else thinks about them! Drunks are bold and uninhibited, because they are under the control of something else. Whatever fear of man the 120 in the Upper Room had *before* was gone, and they were free to move with God. They caused a mighty revival, because they were **N-TOXICATED** with Him!

Make a list of things that may be holding you back from radical leadership. Ask the Lord to N-TOXICATE you with His boldness to lead your team.

N-TRICATELY

| in·tri·cate·ly |

[having many complex interrelating parts or elements;
complicated]
[difficulty in resolving or analyzing]
[hard to understand]

**You do not know what someone else has been through
until you take the time to N-TRICATELY know them.**

Not long ago, we were at lunch with some friends, and they were describing a situation where someone was dealing with serious depression. As we continued in the discussion, something dawned on me: Everything they were saying was also a description of me at the time. It did not take long for me to realize that I, too, was dealing with depression and anxiety. Of course, Cyndy and I immediately prayed, but then we began to research the subject of depression. We discovered two things that contribute to the tendencies towards depression are artificial sweeteners, like diet drinks, and nasal spray. Both of these were a big part of my daily routine. After I removed these from my life, I stopped having anxiety attacks. Who knew? God did—and He revealed it through an **N-TRICATE** conversation with my friends!

*"My frame was not hidden from you when
I was formed in secret and INTRICATELY
and curiously wrought."*

Psalms 139:15 (AMP)

When you understand how we are spiritual, physical, emotional, chemical, electrical, and mental beings, then you can better conceive why someone can be going through so many different challenges all at the same time. Someone on your team might be in a crisis; and in order to help them effectively, you need God's insight to sort out the **N-TRICATE** details of what is really happening. Do not assume you understand. Go to the One who knows every aspect of a person's being, and then you can truly help them.

**Who on your team needs some N-TRICATE
attention today?**

N-TRIGUE

| in·trigue |

[to arouse curiosity]
[attract; captivate]

Your curiosity of life will cause you to be a seeker of wisdom. Let the N-TRIGUE of how the Kingdom of Heaven works captivate your attention.

O nce while working in the control room at Cowboys Stadium, I made it a point to ask questions when my supervisors were around. I could turn on a computer and function well, but this was high-tech stuff. I'm sure my supervisors were tired of all my inquiries, but I endeavored to try new aspects of that computer program every time I was there and was continually learning something new. Eventually, others would ask me how to do something, and I could tell them. At times, people would even call me to fix things, and I could do it over the phone. My **N-TRIGUE** of how that system worked turned into increase of valuable knowledge.

"[Four things of INTRIGUE] Three things are too amazing to me, even four that I cannot understand:"

Proverbs 30:18 (GW)

If your prayer life is a constant repetition of "canned" prayers, your Christianity will eventually start to feel like processed food, full of preservatives. The freshness will be gone. Practice asking God real questions like: "What's wrong with this picture?" "How is this situation supposed to work out?" "What could I do to be better in this situation?" By asking real questions to a real God, you will begin feeling like you have real answers for real situations. Then, you can be a real leader . . . for real! Your **N-TRIGUE** of how God does things will turn into wisdom for every situation.

Write down two things you need to fix on your team. Begin asking God specific questions, letting your N-TRIGUE to know drive you to the answers!

N-TRODUCE

| in·tro·duce |

[to lead or bring in especially for the first time]
[to bring into play]
[to lead to or make known by a formal act, announcement, or recommendation]

Leaders are most often the connectors of ability, wisdom, and opportunity. Be the one who N-TRODUCES others to the big picture!

I n my senior year of high school, I had two best friends, Bruce and Dan. We would go places together and hang out. No matter where we were, we could always be ourselves because of our friendship. They were a year younger than me, so they stayed in Grand Rapids, Michigan, while I went to Texas after graduation. This is where I met the Lord. When I came home for the summer, Bruce introduced me to his Christian friend. We all hung out together, and then we led Bruce to the Lord! I was so nervous, because I had never done that before; but it was such a great privilege. Since that time, I have always been so thankful for any opportunity God gives me to **N-TRODUCE** others to Him.

*"So Paul took his stand in the open space
at the Areopagus and laid it out for them.
'It is plain to see that you Athenians took
your religion seriously. When I arrived
here the other day, I was fascinated with
all the shrines I came across. And then I
found one inscribed, to the God nobody
knows. I'm here to INTRODUCE you to
this God so you can worship intelligently,
know who you're dealing with.'"*

Acts 17:22 (MSG)

When Paul was first brought to the apostles, they had
no idea what to think about the former destroyer of the
Church who had now turned into a super-believer.
Barnabus, knowing the change God had done in Paul's
heart, **N-TRODUCED** him to the other apostles anyways.
This started Paul on a life of **N-TRODUCING** others to
the love of God. Your life is built on your connections to
people who shape you. As you work together and complement
one another's strengths, you will be stronger . . . together.

**Who do you know who needs to be N-TRODUCED to
each other? Make some calls and get it on the calendar to
N-TRODUCE them!**

N-TUITION

| in·tu·i·tion |

[quick and ready insight]
[immediate apprehension or cognition]

You have an inner voice that will tell you the way of success if you learn to tune into it and listen! Take time to develop your N-TUITION.

My sons were teenagers when we started Youth WAVE Church. I was 40 years old and quite removed from all sense of what it meant to be "cool" and captivating of young people's attention. My **N-TUITION** told me to listen to my sons' **N-TUITION**. My ideas would have to pass their "lame" test in order to be implemented. If they said it was a lame idea, it probably was. As a result, we were able to create a unique church that did all types of cool and relatable things. One thing we created was an innovative "videoke" before anyone else hardly knew what it was! As a result, we were able to help a bunch of young people stand when others were falling.

"Who gives INTUITION to the heart and instinct to the mind? Who is wise enough to count all the clouds? Who can tilt the water jars of heaven?"

Job 38:36-37 (NLT)

Jesus did not come and take everything over. Instead, He took 12 men and shaped them into the leaders they needed to be to build His Church. Jesus had heavenly **N-TUITION**, while the disciples had fish **N-TUITION**. It took both to get the job done. Listen to your inner voice, even if it is telling you to get **N-TUITION** input from others on your team. It could save you time, money, and headaches—and keep you from looking lame!

Who on your team do you need to tune into today? Use your leadership N-TUITION.

N-TENSE

| in·tense |

[existing in an extreme degree]
[marked by or expressive of great zeal, energy,
determination, or concentration]

**The most successful people in the world have an
N-TENSITY in one particular area. N-TENSIFY your
calling by focusing on it!**

Cyndy and I love getting together with leaders and
brainstorming about ministry, life, and challenges.
Consulting and helping pastors and leaders process
where they have been and where they are going has been
one of our greatest joys in the ministry. We can get so
excited in the middle of our conversations, especially when
we are trying to process a year's worth of experiences in one
concentrated get-together—*that* is almost too **N-TENSE**.

Think of it as taking concentrated orange juice, freeze-
drying it into powder, and then snorting it. That is a bunch
of Vitamin C in a way that would make your head spin. (We
have to gauge ourselves and pace the brainstorming, so it
doesn't hurt the brain.) It's amazing how many people God
has allowed us the privilege of encouraging with a holy
N-TENSITY!

> *"Rejoice and be glad at such a time and exult and leap for joy, for behold, your reward is rich and great and strong and INTENSE and abundant in heaven; for even so their forefathers treated the prophets."*

Luke 6:23 (AMP)

Many times, leaders on the front lines of innovation get overwhelmed by the circumstances such creativity produces. When people don't understand the very ideas that release life-giving change, they tear them down. Jesus had a prescription for that. When **N-TENSE** persecution comes, rejoice with **N-TENSITY** for the **N-TENSE** reward that is coming your way! The more **N-TENSE** the persecution, the more concentrated your reward will be. Make the mental and emotional adjustments necessary. Instead of being **N-TENSELY** depressed, get **N-TENSELY** happy and enjoy the fact that Jesus is excited about what He is going to do for you!

Proclaim every conversation you have today N-TENSELY, like you are telling it to 1,000 people.

N-THUSIASTIC

| en·thu·si·as·tic |

[filled with or marked by enthusiasm]
[devoted; eager]
[passionate about something]

Your passion in leadership should be contagious. Develop a speech to give yourself every morning to charge your N-THUSIASM for your mission, your vision, and your team.

B oth of our sons made really good grades all through school. Ryan has the ability to really focus on projects and designs websites and ad campaigns for many businesses and ministries. I attribute some of this to his kindergarten teacher. She was amazing, always smiling, and had one of those voices that made every student want to do whatever she said because it sounded like so much FUN! Her bubbly personality and pleasant tone made Ryan look forward to attending school each day and made learning an exciting adventure. From kindergarten on, he has always enjoyed learning. She was full of **N-THUSIASM**, and it created an **N-THUSIASTIC** atmosphere!

"God gave each of us different gifts; if it is leadership, lead ENTHUSIASTICALLY."

Romans 12:7-8 (GW)

As a leader, you set the tone of your team—good or bad. Is everyone on your team excited to get together or do they dread it? Does everyone jump in because it feels like an adventure or do they come up with excuses to not be involved because they are burned out? Let Jesus lead you into His daily adventures, as you walk in the reality of Him. This is what keeps your leadership fresh and **N-THUSIASTIC.** En-Theo means "God in you." Release God in you, and your team will respond to your passion to lead them!

Let every word you speak today be bursting with N-THUSIASM and see what happens.

N-TITLE

| en·ti·tle |

[to give a title to; designate]
To furnish with proper grounds for seeking or claiming
something]

Everybody does something well. Look for the good in the members of your team and give encouraging words to those who are N-TITLED!

When I was 13, I picked up a plastic, battery-powered toy guitar that my brother had forgotten about, and began to play the song "Crimson and Clover" over and over on the one string that remained. That was soon followed by a $9 acoustic guitar from Montgomery Ward. By Christmas that year, I opened my first electric guitar and amp. I fell in love with the guitar and played in several bands in high school. The only problem was, I was so insecure that playing in front of people terrified me. One day in Bible college, I was worshipping God by myself with the doors shut, when one of my roommates peeked in and told me how great I sounded and that I should sing in front of the whole school. "Yeah, right!" I thought to myself, dismissing the idea. But, the seed was planted, and within a year his prophecy had come to pass.

His words of encouragement began to **N-TITLE** me out of my insecurities.

> *"Don't hold back anything good from those who are ENTITLED to it when you have the power to do so."*
>
> **Proverbs 3:27 (GW)**

Imagine if Jesus had not asked those fishermen to follow Him. Imagine if He had not restored Peter after He had denied even knowing Jesus. The moments where specific words are spoken that change our course in life are like memorials in our destiny. Every one of us can point back to a turning point in our lives where someone spoke some words, and it affected our choices. If you see something good in someone, tell them. It might be an opportunity to give them something that God believes they are **N-TITLED** to!

Find three people today who deserve a compliment.
N-TITLE them to go further!

N-DELIBLE

| in·del·i·ble |

[that cannot be removed, washed away, or erased]
[lasting]

Stepping into a leadership position is like getting a tattoo—
once it's on you, it never comes off . . . EVER! God's image
on your life is N-DELIBLE.

During the 10 years I pastored Youth WAVE Church, we targeted a specific group of people based on age and interest. Not to far away, another cultural church called Deliverance Bible Church came on the scene. (They now meet in our first facility) This church was pioneered by Pastor Cleetus and Lady Nichole Adrian. Part of their goal is to reach people who love Jesus with all of their hearts and express it through their tattoos and their super passionate, loud praise and worship. The underground crowd this church ministers to each week is filled with some of the most amazing Christians I have ever met. Their commitment to Christ is as **N-DELIBLE** as their tattoos! They have churches in Detroit, Michigan; Hollywood, California; New Orleans, Louisiana; Seattle, Washington; Spokane, Washington; Brazil, and Columbia. Pastor Cleetus and his family are also laying the groundwork for new ministry opportunities in Paris, France. They are making an **N-DELIBLE** mark for Christ all around the world.

> *"Behold, I have INDELIBLY imprinted (tattooed a picture of) you on the palm of each of My hands; [O Zion] your walls are continually before Me."*
>
> **Isaiah 49:16 (AMP)**

When the prophet Elijah called Elisha into the ministry, the young man, Elisha, chopped up his wood plow he worked the fields with and used it as fuel to roast his ox. Then, he said goodbye to his family and left. When it was time for Elijah to go to Heaven, Elisha told him he wanted twice the anointing that God had given Elijah. After the chariot from Heaven took Elijah, Elisha took his mentor's mantle and struck the river saying, "Where is the God of Elijah?" and the waters parted. Elisha walked like, talked like, and performed miracles like his master. Their names are even similar! If you saw Elisha, you would immediately know he was Elijah's protégé. That kind of influence does not rub off. Its mark is **N-DELIBLE.**

What N-DELIBLE leadership impression are you leaving on others?

N-TERROGATE

| in·ter·ro·gate |

[to question formally and systematically]
[to give or send out a signal to (as a transponder) for
triggering an appropriate response]

**Believe it or not, you have been N-TERROGATED
before either by your parents, your girl/boyfriend, or your
boss. Learn how to ask the right questions and become an
expert at bringing out the best in others.**

The receptionist told me, "He says he's a friend of yours," even though I did not recognize His name. "He doesn't have an appointment, but wondered if he could see you for a few minutes." As one of the pastors at a church, I wanted to be accommodating; so I went to the lobby, and we greeted one another and shook hands. Then he followed me to my office. He quickly shut the door behind me and apologized for the charade. As it turned out, he worked for the government and was investigating a young man in our youth group who was applying for a military job on a nuclear submarine. Come to find out, there was nothing wrong with this young man; they were just concerned about his relationship with another teen friend who had been in some trouble with the law. You have to be careful who you hang around! People find out everything about you if they **N-TERROGATE** you long enough.

> *"The soldiers who were about to INTER-*
> *ROGATE Paul quickly withdrew when*
> *they heard he was a Roman Citizen."*

Acts 22:29a (NLT)

Paul loved being **N-TERROGATED**. For him, it was like being a guest on a talk show—another opportunity to share the Gospel! Since it was the religious leaders who were accusing him, the soldiers must have assumed that it was just another religious matter. They never dreamed he was a Roman Citizen from birth, which meant they could be sentenced to death if they but laid a hand on him. The more they asked, the more they knew . . . and the more Paul had the opportunity to influence them. Sometimes, you have to get serious to find out who someone really is!

Pick someone on your team who you only know on the surface and spend some time with them. Conduct a holy N-TERROGATION!

N-TACT

| in·tact |

[untouched especially by anything that harms or diminishes]
[entire]
[having no relevant component removed or destroyed]

When the pressure is on, you will find your level of leadership strength. When things get tough, you will emerge N-TACT!

One summer while driving in our van on a ministry tour, Cyndy and I camped out with our two boys in between speaking engagements. (This was a money issue, not an exploration of the wilderness issue.) We were in Canada at a campground and my side began to hurt. The pain grew so badly that I asked Cyndy to take me to the hospital. She knew it was serious! We drove up to the emergency room and left our van in the driveway while we went inside to see the doctor, because our boys were asleep in the back. At one point, Cyndy went outside to check on them around 4 a.m., and they were watching comics on TV. Jesse said, "Mom, we woke up and thought somebody stole us!" This, along with our travel, and me in the emergency room was almost too many emotions for Cyndy to handle. It took all she had to stay **N-TACT!** After my examination and

X-rays, the doctor said I had just pulled a muscle under my rib cage, and I needed to go and check into a hotel room to sleep for two to three days. Thank God, I was still **N-TACT!**

> *"Now, that the worst is over, we're pleased we can report that we've come out of this with conscience and faith INTACT, and can face the world . . . It was God who kept us focused on Him."*
>
> **1 Corinthians 1:12-13 (MSG)**

In Daniel chapter three, there were three men who refused to bow down and worship the golden image which King Nebuchadnezzar had built. They boldly declared their faith in God and were thrown in a fiery furnace. While in the fire, they stayed **N-TACT** and were seen walking around with someone who looked like the Son of God! The king brought them out of the fire and He promoted these three guys—Shadrach, Meshach, and Abednego—and declared their God was real. They kept their faith strong and God turned the nation around. The lesson to learn is: Do not be a limp leader. Make a strong stand with and for your team no matter what the odds. Come out of the fire **N-TACT.**

Identify an area that needs you to take a strong stand and work on making your team more N-TACT!

N-VADE

| in·vade |

[to enter for conquest or plunder]
[to encroach upon; infringe]
[to spread over or into as if invading; permeate]

Stir up your spirit to N-VADE and take the success which belongs to you and your team!

We developed a program called, "Do the Daniel Thing!" to stir up young people to pray for their schools. We were equipping teens to be like Daniel and his three friends who stood up for God in a godless environment. The t-shirt we made to go with the program had the verse *"Daniel purposed in His heart that he would not defile himself."* (Daniel 1:8) One young lady wore her t-shirt to school one day and another student stopped her and frantically said, "Your shirt is convicting me!" This was not really the reaction she was looking for, but it presented an opportunity to be a light in a dark place. Little did she know that the raw power of God's written Word on her t-shirt would **N-VADE** people's hearts!

"You are crossing the Jordan River to INVADE and take the land that God, your God is giving you. Be vigilant. Observe all the regulations and rules I am setting before you today."

Deuteronomy 11:31 (MSG)

The world is waiting for someone to stand out in the crowd. Many rise up and represent the Babylon mentality, but few will shine like the sun and bring the love of God into realms that have been without it for too long. So often, today's leaders try and blend in and make everybody happy. John the Baptist stood out. The disciples stood out. Jesus stood out. They **N-VADED** their generation with good news while there was political and religious bondage everywhere. Will you be the leader who heads up the charge into the world of opportunities that awaits you? It is time to **N-VADE!**

What worlds can you go N-VADE today and take God's ability with you to make a difference? Your job? Your school? Your family?

N-VENTORY

| in·ven·to·ry |

[an itemized list of current assets]
[survey; summary]
[the quantity of goods or materials on hand; stock]

Jesus had an unlimited supply of creative ability. Have you checked your creative N-VENTORY lately?

They told me I had 30 minutes to speak to the student body of a Christian high school in Australia. There must have been over 500 teens there that day. This chapel meeting was just before lunch, so I knew my timing had to be precise. The students would be hungry and would want to get out of there. I do not remember the message, just that only about 10 kids came forward at the end for prayer. The microphone was still on as I prayed for one, then the next, and so on. The prophetic prayers I was praying over these young men and women must have hit a nerve because 10 turned into 20, which turned into 30, and so on. Kids who had gone to lunch heard what was going on and came back for prayer. The 30-minute session ended two hours later, and everyone was full. I had never met any of these students before, but I reached into the **N-VENTORY** of Heaven and found the supply!

"But he was quite serious. 'How many loaves of bread do you have? Take an INVENTORY.' That didn't take long. 'Five,' they said, 'plus two fish.'"

Mark 6:38 (MSG)

Jesus and His team had been ministering for days, and so many people were healed and delivered, but they were all hungry and had no food. The disciples managed to find a few fish and loaves of bread but not nearly enough to meet the demand. But then, Jesus reached into His heavenly **N-VENTORY** and multiplied them, feeding everyone around plus leaving leftovers! Not only was Jesus concerned for the spiritual needs of the people, His care for their daily needs was displayed loud and clear. He taught them the truth and demonstrated the love.

When you run out of ideas and words to inspire, that is when you tap into His **N-VENTORY** and start giving the living bread. You might not feel like you have anything to say or any life-changing speeches to give, but He does. Sometimes, you just need to open your mouth and get out of the way. He has the **N-VENTORY** . . . all you have to do is deliver!

What leadership gifts are you holding in your N-VENTORY? Put yourself in a position today to draw them out.

N-VOLUNTARY

| in·vol·un·tary |

[done contrary to or without choice]
[compulsory]
[not subject to the control of the will; reflex]

Leadership should be as natural as a heartbeat. Success should be an N-VOLUNTARY response.

I recently heard that the game, Ping Pong, was really good for your brain. There is something about the focus of seeing the moving ball and your brain sending signals to your arm to hit the ball—the way to hit it, how hard, and how fast—that can keep your brain sharp. I have noticed that if you play enough Ping Pong, your reactionary reflexes take over; and when you play, it is almost an **N-VOLUNTARY** response like a heartbeat or breathing. It also helps your eye-hand coordination to respond to everything else—like catching a fly with chopsticks!

"But it has been my wish to do nothing about it without first consulting you and getting your consent, in order that your benevolence might not seem to be the result of INVOLUNTARY pressure on your part."

Philemon 1:14 (Paraphrased)

Onesimus, a man who had made himself very valuable to Paul while he was in prison, had apparently created a negative rapport with Philemon, a wealthy slave owner who hosted a church in his home. Paul sent Onesimus back to Philemon, and it almost seems as if he was checking to see what Philemon's response would be to him. He was seeing if Philemon's generosity and obedience had developed to the point of it becoming an **N-VOLUNTARY** response, like, "Of course I will receive Him. I'll do whatever you ask!" Paul wanted to make sure that he was not causing additional pressure for him, while making known what He believed to be the will of God for everyone involved. When you treat your leaders right, they develop the proper response to every change in direction and grow to become servant leaders like Jesus Himself!

Develop three ways you can train your team to have an N-VOLUNTARY response to forward motion.

N-VITING

| in·vi·ting |

[attractive]
[appealing]

Leaders are approachable, connectable, and N-VITING. They make new people feel like they are part of the team.

I love it when people **N-VITE** us to dinner by asking if they can take us out and then have a specific night and time. It is decisive and direct and leaves no room for misunderstanding. When people say, "Let's get together sometime!" the "sometime" usually never comes. There is an art to **N-VITING** people. If you **N-VITE** someone to church, be specific and tell them, "Be there this Sunday," and tell them what time and the specific spot where you will meet them. Then, be early and save them seats. If you want to really amp it up, tell them what the dress code is—Sunday best or casual—and tell them what time you will be picking them up! They can still say no, but when you are that detailed, eventually they will make the appointment, and it could be divine.

"Hezekiah sent word to all Israel and Judah, INVITING them to come to the temple of the Lord in Jerusalem and celebrate the Passover."

2 Chronicles 30:1 (NIV)

When there is purpose and a cause, people want to get involved. If someone thinks everyone is going to be involved, they will want to be involved, too. Hezekiah was not trying out the latest church growth formula; there was a move of God going on, and he wanted everyone to get in on it. In verse 26 of this same chapter, it says there was great joy in Jerusalem because nothing like this had happened since King Solomon, so everyone was excited. You, too, are an awesome leader and have a great thing going. Get excited about what you are doing and **N-VITE** everyone to be involved and to be a part of it. Your whole persona becomes **N-VITING** when you believe in your team enough to **N-VITE** others.

Practice N-VITING everyone you see today.

N-VINCIBLE

| in·vin·ci·ble |

[incapable of being conquered, overcome, or subdued]

Leaders lead the charge, knowing they are the first into battle, the last to leave, and their influence is N-VINCIBLE.

We took four of our grandkids to the pool, and we wondered if we were going to be able to keep up with them. The two oldest were fine; they swim well and know their way around. Then, there is our two year-old granddaughter who is very clingy and keeps herself from trouble. At the opposite end of the spectrum is our four year-old granddaughter, who thinks she is **N-VINCIBLE**. While holding her in the deep water, she started squirming like a catfish trying to get loose, so she could swim away. But, there was only one problem . . . she had not quite learned how to swim! It took everything I had to keep up with her fearless attitude. In her mind, that girl is **N-VINCIBLE**; and she does not have an "off" switch!

"The Lord God is my strength, my personal bravery, and my INVINCIBLE army. He makes my feet like hinds feet and will make me to walk and make spiritual progress up on my high places (of trouble, suffering, or responsibility)."

Habakkuk 3:19 (AMP)

David had this kind of confidence in His God. When a lion took a lamb from his flock, David struck it and took it back. When David faced Goliath, Goliath trash-talked him, telling him what he was going to do with his dead body. That was all the motivation David needed. The undersized, red-haired kid from Bethlehem opened his mouth and what came out was bigger than any giant. David told Goliath what he was going to do to him, what the result would be, and declared that this would bring glory to God and establish God's people in the earth! God had to back him up. When you know your God is **N-VINCIBLE**, you become fearless. Lead with fearless confidence, knowing that God will take care of you and your team no matter what!

What charge do you need to lead your team into to be an N-VINCIBLE influence on the world?

N-VIGORATE

| in·vig·o·rate |

[to give life and energy to]
[animate; stimulate]

Be a refreshing force in the lives of those on your team. Take what you have and make it N-VIRGORATING!

I was born and raised in Michigan. The winters were dark and cold there; so when springtime came, we were ready. Frozen in my memories is the **N-VIGORATING** first swim of the summer. We were all ready for spring, but the pool still thought it was winter because it was ice cold. It did not matter to us though, as we attacked the chilly depths with an attitude. We would not be denied one moment of summer and enjoyed this **N-VIGORATING** moment as if it were our only chance.

"Good–tempered leaders INVIGORATE lives; they're like spring rain and sunshine.

Proverbs 16:15 (MSG)

All you really possess are the "now" moments! You can either use these opportunities to produce life and excitement for the future, or you can waste the chance and do nothing. The sad truth is that most people are just waiting to wake up from a boring existence. However, you are not like most people! Just like a hot cup of coffee in the morning or splashing cold water on your face or jumping into an ice cold pool, you can wake yourself up to the fact that Jesus came to give you life more abundantly. Out of that excitement and anticipation, you can bring life to your team. **N-VIGORATE** everyone around you about what God is doing and is getting ready to do for you. Go ahead, jump in! The water is **N-VIGORATING!**

Who can you N-VIGORATE today?

N-VESTIGATE

| in·ves·ti·gate |

[to observe or study by close examination and
systematic inquiry]
[to conduct an official inquiry]

Leaders know . . . because leaders ask. They find out
direction from God, solutions to problems, and strategies
for success. Become a private N-VESTIGATOR.

When Cyndy and I were traveling and conducting our Warfare Weekends, a church would host the seminar, and we invited other congregations in the area to join us. We would **N-VESTIGATE** and research the history, the culture, and the mood of that particular location. Cyndy found one city where the military base was preparing to deploy some troops, therefore we knew how to pray and prepare for the meetings. While driving into another city, I found myself getting extremely impatient and angry with our boys, which was very unusual. We **N-VESTIGATED** and learned that the city lead the nation in child abuse that year. We taught how to **N-VESTIGATE** and recognize strongholds in a city that could be affected through prayer and also how to begin to change the spiritual atmosphere of a place.

"So I turned my mind to understand, to INVESTIGATE and to search out wisdom and the scheme of things, and to understand the stupidity of wickedness and the madness of folly."

Ecclesiastes 7:25 (NIV)

When Joshua sent two spies to **N-VESTIGATE** Jericho, they quickly learned that the reputation of God's people already caused fear to spring up in the hearts of this well-fortified community. They heard about the Red Sea opening up and did not know what to expect. Learning that the enemy was already afraid was the information they needed to take away all doubt. I am sure that the extra confidence this provided eliminated a whole lot of complaining and second-guessing. Because they **N-VESTIGATED**, they were armed with the knowledge that God had gone before them and prepared the way.

Make a list of questions you need God to answer, and spend some time N-VESTIGATING the answers from the Bible today!

N-VEST

| in·vest |

[to use, give, or devote]
[to furnish or endow with power]
[to put money to use]

Leaders have a vision for the future of their team and N-VEST in their success.

When we minister on the road, we usually set up a book table to offer books, t-shirts, and recorded messages. Early on in our travels, we discovered witness bracelets containing five colors—each representing a different aspect of salvation through Christ—and saw this as a great opportunity for our sons to get involved. Those bracelets proved to be a great opportunity to share Jesus for whoever wore one. Making these bracelets was fairly simple to do; and our son, Jesse, started his witness bracelet business. Soon, he hired his younger brother, Ryan, to help make them. All the money from the bracelet sales went into their bank accounts. Starting to **N-VEST** as children gave them a real sense of financial stability, which they both enjoy today. They prosper, give, save, and spend with the wisdom they learned at an early age.

"Before he left, he called ten of his servants and gave them ten coins. He said to his servants, 'INVEST the money until I come back.'"

Luke 19:13 (GW)

Being **N-VESTMENT**-minded instead of "spend crazy" makes all the difference in the world. Learning to be excited about **N-VESTING** money that turns a profit for you, instead of being thrilled at just buying stuff, is vital if you are going to progress financially. Treat yourself to a savings account; so that when it is time to buy something you really need, you pay cash for it and save thousands of dollars in interest over your lifetime. Take what God has given you—financially, socially, and spiritually—and use it wisely. **N-VEST** your time, attention, and money into what really matters, and let others collect stuff. You will end up richer in every way!

Make an N-VESTMENT chart. Organize what you can N-VEST in your savings account, in your marriage, and in the morale of your team!

N-VARIABLE

| in·vari·able |

[not changing or capable of change]
[constant]

Leaders lead. They exhibit N-VARIABLE peace and confidence in the plans and directions they are taking their team.

Growing up with two brothers and two sisters, we had to share a lot of things, including bedrooms. My older brother and I slept in a bunk bed with me taking the top bunk. I was such a sound sleeper that, from time to time, I would fall out of the top bed onto the floor, and I would not even wake up. Sometimes we would stay up and watch scary movies on TV, like *Frankenstein* or *Dracula*, and I would have no problem going right to sleep afterwards. My brother, on the other hand, would stay awake and make sure no monsters snuck into our room. Now, after being married and having children, I am much more aware of things and wake up easily. Thinking back on those days of nocturnal bliss reminds me of the **N-VARIABLE** peace that God fills our hearts with, no matter what is going on around us.

"You will guard him and keep him in perfect and INVARIABLE peace whose mind is stayed on You, because he commits himself to You, leans on You, and hopes confidently in You."

Isaiah 62:3 (Paraphrased)

When Herod killed the apostle, James, and saw that it pleased the people, he proceeded to have the apostle Peter arrested and ordered his death. The night before Peter's scheduled execution, the Church gathered to pray; and God sent an angel into the prison where Peter was being held. Peter was so sound asleep that the angel had to kick him to wake him up, so they could get out of there. Every door in front of them opened by itself, and the angel led him out of prison . . . but Peter was still half asleep. When they were completely out, the angel disappeared. It was not until then that Peter realized it was not a dream.

Now, I don't know about you, but the night before my execution, I am not sure how well I would be able to sleep! Thank God for His perfect, unchanging, **N-VARIABLE** peace.

List any areas of unrest in your group and construct a plan to lead your team with N-VARIABLE peace!

N-VALUABLE

| in·valu·able |

[valuable beyond estimation]
[priceless]

Leadership lessons are N-VALUABLE. You cannot put a price on eternal experiences.

While attending some meetings at a minister's conference, there was an altar call for anyone wanting more of God. I went forward because we needed some breakthroughs to go to the next step in our life and ministry. The host pastor's wife suddenly came up to me, put something in my hand, and whispered in my ear, "Make sure Cyndy gets this!" I stuck it in my pocket and did not even look at it. Later that evening, in the car, I gave it to Cyndy. She was so overwhelmed that she began to cry. It was a beautiful, one-of-a-kind diamond ring set in gold! A unique piece of jewelry, it had 12 round diamonds along the edge of its V-shape and a marquise diamond in the center. Cyndy was amazed, not only that she would give her such a valuable gift, but because we had been through so many things together with this couple and God's grace kept our friendship alive. The ring itself was valuable, but it became **N-VALUABLE** to Cyndy because of the miracle of our relationship. Whenever Cyndy looks at this ring, she prays for this couple. She could never give it away because of what it represents—friendship!

> *"Honor, esteem, and make INVALUABLE your father and your mother—this is the commandment with a promise."*
>
> **Ephesians 6:2 (Paraphrased)**

Just before Jesus suffered and died, Mary anointed Him with fragrant oil, which at the time was worth a year's wages. Judas was upset because he wanted to sell the oil for a profit, but Mary gave her best. Her gift, combined with the gesture in which it was given, became an **N-VALUABLE** part of the redemption story. The oil with which she anointed Jesus created such an aroma that it stayed in the minds of everyone who came near Him within the next 24 hours. Her gift was **N-VALUABLE**. As a leader, be mindful of performing significant acts of kindness and support to your team members. These acts will become memorable pieces of their life story.

What one-of-a-kind, N-VALUABLE memory can you create with your team that will live with them forever?

N-UNDATE

| in·un·date |

[to cover with a flood; overflow]
[overwhelm]

The leadership of Jesus N-UNDATED a small group of men. They overflowed with the energy of eternity.

We live next to a drainage ditch that the city built to carry off excess water when we have heavy rains. It has a certain capacity because of its size. It is about eight feet deep and 15 feet wide. There is a bridge at the corner of our lot that goes right over the top of it. When we have an abundance of rain in a short period of time and the water rises rapidly, it floods the ditch and the bridge. Once, the water pressure was so powerful that it pushed the asphalt completely off of the concrete bridge supports. Several times, I have called the local police to set up barricades to keep people from driving across the bridge when it is **N-UNDATED** with rushing water. It is a powerful display of nature that happens right outside our house.

218

"Behold, He restrains the waters and they dry up; and he sends them out and they INUNDATE the earth."

Job 12:15 (NAS)

The apostle Paul kept himself busy by traveling from place to place, raising up pastors and leaders for the churches he started. One time, though, he found himself in a very strategic place. It was at the School of Tyrannus, which had the same dynamic as a university today. This was a place where people from all over Asia would come to hear what was new and to learn from others. Paul stayed there for two years, preaching the Gospel and discipling converts. Because of the constant stream of people pouring through that one spot, all of Asia heard the Word of God. As a result, Asia was **N-UNDATED** with the Gospel due to the fact that Paul planted himself at the source which flowed out to that entire region.

Examine your teams flow and re-position things, if need be, so they can be **N-UNDATED** with excitement for the future!

N-TERMITTENT

| in·ter·mit·tent |

[coming and going at intervals]
[recurrent; rhythmic]

Once you have tasted true leadership, nothing else compares. You will **N-TERMITTENTLY** come back to it over and over again.

My new favorite flavor of Blue Bell® ice cream is Key Lime Pie. It is much smoother than a piece of really good key lime pie, without the twang—and it's ice cream! When we brought home our first half gallon, it was just too good to leave alone. It was like the whole thing was just sitting there waiting on me; so spoonful by spoonful, a small cup here and a small cup there, I quickly ate the entire thing. Cyndy opened up the freezer and asked me, "Hey, who ate all the ice cream?" Since we did not have a dog or kids to blame, I had to take full responsibility. The entire half gallon was gone as I **N-TERMITTENTLY** enjoyed it!

> *"You gave me no kiss, but she from the moment I came in has not ceased (INTERMITTENTLY) to kiss my feet tenderly and caressingly."*

Luke 7:45 (AMP)

Jesus once accepted a dinner invitation at a Pharisee's house. While He ate, a sinner woman crashed the party and started washing His feet with her tears, wiping them with her hair, and anointing Him with very expensive oils. The religious leader was appalled that Jesus would let this unclean woman touch Him at all, but her repentance, sincerity, and hunger for the life-changing love of Jesus would not let her stop. The minute she thought her expression of love was complete, she would break out in tears and start washing the Master's feet all over again. (I have always said this woman was following shampoo instructions—lather, rinse, repeat—over and over.) In the same way, when you develop an appetite for His unconditional, transforming love, you cannot get enough. You have to keep coming back and getting more and more of Jesus. Like the sinner woman, when you have tasted heaven, you **N-TERMITTENTLY** have to have more.

Be N-TERMITTENT with your success. Keep coming back to reading, speaking, and practicing true leadership!

N-TENT

| in·tent |

[the act or fact of intending]
[purpose]
[a usually clearly formulated or planned intention;
aim; meaning, significance]

Your N-TENT should be for your team to connect, grow, and advance towards the success of the entire team. Check your N-TENT.

C hristmas with Cyndy's family is always a crazy, blessed affair. Her sister and brother-in-law, Brad and Denise Howard, host the annual Gosnell family Christmas party. There are over 44 of us, and the number grows each year. It is a lot of work for Brad and Denise, but they love it. Their **N-TENT** is for everyone to re-connect, so they set the tables with place cards and group everyone according to their age. Great grandchildren have cute paper plates, plastic silverware and cups with tops, and even chocolate candy just for them. Grandchildren who are teenagers have cool Christmas plates and glasses with lots of space for their games and cell phones. The grown-up's table is occupied by Cyndy's mom, Elna Gosnell, and her four daughters. We use the family Christmas China and real silverware and glasses. Eating is about a two-hour ordeal, then we open presents and top off the celebration with great desserts and coffee. Brad and Denise do a marvelous job of bringing us all together, which is exactly their **N-TENT** for the occasion.

> *"His INTENT was that now, through the church, the manifold wisdom of God should be made known to the rulers and authorities in the heavenly realms."*
>
> **Ephesians 3:10 (NIV)**

When we were youth pastors, we made it a priority to have our leaders come together once a week for pre-service prayer. Our **N-TENT** was to give them a safe environment to open up if they were dealing with a difficult situation or going through a tough time. We did not want to assume that everyone was okay or expect the leadership team to handle everything on their own. If they were being attacked with depression or temptation, we wanted to help each other. Sometimes, if the **N-TENT** is *"just"* to have a great service, we miss the opportunity to be a support system to those closest to us. After praying for each other's needs, they would be so pumped up and ready to be a blessing to those coming to the service. Strong, healthy leaders are what make a great team!

Make it your N-TENT this week to build up your team!

N-STRUMENT

| in·stru·ment |

[a device used to produce music]
[a means whereby something is achieved, performed, or furthered]
[implement; one designed for precision work]

Leaders learn how to recognize, utilize, and harmonize gifts in others. Rally the N-STRUMENTS and make some noise!

Early in our youth pastoring years, I switched from leading worship with an acoustic 12-string guitar to an electric guitar. I chose a Telecaster (appropriately named) and our youth group doubled. Many guitars later, I was looking for an **N-STRUMENT** that would fit in any setting, and I found (as you probably guessed) another Telecaster! This one had Tele pick-ups, a Stratocaster pick-up, and a Fishman power bridge. In other words, it could be two very distinct sounding electric guitars, as well as an acoustic guitar, all in one package. This **N-STRUMENT** does everything I need it to do.

"But the Lord said to Him, 'Go for he is a chosen INSTRUMENT of mine to carry my name before the Gentiles and kings and the children of Israel.'"

Acts 9:15 (ESV)

When God was looking for an **N-STRUMENT**, He noticed Saul—born a Roman, raised in the Jewish culture, and trained as a religious leader. Saul's unique set of qualifications had him persecuting the Church, but God saw his potential and sent Jesus to give him a supernatural, life-altering encounter on the road to Damascus. He was transformed into Paul, and God chose him as an **N-STRUMENT** for the Gospel that could fit into any setting. Paul was specifically gifted to do three different things: (1.) reach the Gentiles with the Gospel, (2.) influence kings, and (3.) minister to God's people. As a leader, be willing to look beyond where people are in their present state and see what God sees in them. Then, you can help unlock their God-given potential, so they can be an **N-STRUMENT** in His hands!

What N-STRUMENTS for success do you see in the members of your team?

N-TERCHANGE

| in·ter·change |

[to put each of (two things] in the place of the other]
[exchange]
[to change places mutually]

Leaders are selfless. They create an N-TERCHANGE of agreement because their vision is for the whole team.

I have found two major deterrents to selfishness. The first is marriage. When you alter your lifestyle to include someone else, you share everything, and shape your personalities to be a couple instead of two individuals. The second is having children. Your time and attention are dominated by your creation. The first is by choice as you **N-TERCHANGE** vows and make promises to live for your spouse. The second is the result of that **N-TERCHANGE**. Two become one, you multiply, and selfishness goes out the window . . . if you are doing it right.

"Isaac laid out a feast and they ate and drank together. Early in the morning they INTERCHANGED oaths. Then Isaac said goodbye, and they parted as friends."

Genesis 26:30-31 (Paraphrased)

Isaac had a covenant mindset that He received from his father, Abraham. When you make a covenant agreement with someone, you share what you have and who you are with that person (or group of people). This means you will be mindful to help care for them, do things for them, and protect them for the rest of your life. Look at the covenant God made with you through Jesus. His promise is to look out for you, provide for you, and protect you. He does so totally unselfishly, putting His Word and integrity on the line in an **N-TERCHANGE** of promises which He cannot break. When you think about God's promises, it helps you be less selfish and inspires you to share and care more about the relationships He has entrusted to you!

N-TERCHANGE promises with your team today. Promise your commitment to each other's success!

N-TERACT

| in·ter·act |

[to act upon one another]
[to collaborate; merge; network]

Leaders learn to N-TERACT wherever they are and train their team to be spiritually flexible.

One day, I was praying about how to help people not be affected by outside influences and this popped up in my heart: "Keep the hose turned on." It was a simple, visual image which illustrated to me that as long as Believers keep the flow going outward, nothing else can clog the life-giving stream that God desires to pour through us. Bugs and debris cannot clog a hose that is always on. The problems, pressures, and persecutions of life cannot get in you if you are living full force. If you read the Word as if you are searching for the solution to the world's problems, your hose is on. If you pray like you are saving an entire nation, your hose is on. If you daily seek out people to bless, encourage, and pray for, your hose is on. Your **N-TERACTION** with God and man should always be "on."

228

"He began to INTERACT with the Jews and Gentile God—worshipers in the synagogue. He also addressed whoever happened to be in the marketplace each day."

Acts 17:17 (CEB)

Paul was a ministry machine going somewhere to happen! His heart was full because of the grace God had given Him. Everywhere Paul went, he **N-TERACTED** with all kinds of people, winning them to Christ and raising up leaders for the churches he pioneered. Surrounded by persecution and opposition, he was never afraid to engage in an **N-TERACTION**, no matter who it was. Paul always kept the hose turned on and watered every person he met. The lesson is simple: Keep the hose on! **N-TERACTION** with God and then with your team will keep the flow open.

What clogs need to be removed to open up healthy N-TERACTION on your team?

N-TEGRITY

| in·teg·ri·ty |

[firm adherence to a code of especially moral or artistic values; incorruptibility]
[an unimpaired condition; soundness]
[the quality or state of being complete or undivided; completeness]

Leaders create disciples by discipline. Spiritual N-TEGRITY produces consistent success.

At City WAVE Church, we had the WAVEmakers Leadership program which included an accountability report that all of our leaders had to complete and turn in each week. Some of the questions they had to answer were: Did you read your Bible every day? Did you pray every day? Did you live a holy and godly lifestyle this week—which meant they did not gossip or create division, go to an "R" rated movie, drink alcohol, or cross the line in a relationship? This not only gave our leaders a reason for *living on purpose* with **N-TEGRITY**, but also gave us the opportunity to be a support system and pray with them when they were going through a tough time. Many times, one of the leaders would come to me and say, "I was going to do something this week, but then realized I couldn't because my **N-TEGRITY** would be at stake on my Accountability Report." The purpose of the program was to create discipline using scriptural guidelines. Today, more than ever, God is holding all of us accountable to live in **N-TEGRITY!**

"Your job is to teach them the rules and instructions to show them how to live, what to do. And then you need to keep a sharp eye out for competent men who fear God—men of INTEGRITY—and appoint them as leaders over groups."

Exodus 18:20-21 (MSG)

Moses was trying to lead the Children of Israel by himself when his wise father-in-law shared some wisdom. It was a simple plan of training leaders, teaching them the rules, and instructing them in the way they were to live. When they were ready, Moses was to release these leaders to help get the job done. As a leader, you have to be careful not to fall into pride and start believing that you do not have to follow the guidelines or can live outside of a disciplined lifestyle. God is not looking for perfect leaders, just those willing to follow Him and do their best—alongside others on His team. I used to think it was only the big decisions that mattered; but the older I get, I realize it is the small day-to-day decisions that keep me on the clear path God has for me and my future. Having people around you who can speak into your life, pray with you, and hold you accountable can keep you going in the right direction. As a leader, you have to *fear God*, which means you honor Him and His commandments, and you are a person of **N-TEGRITY**. That strategy worked for Moses, and it still works today!

Develop a plan for your team that will reinforce the N-TEGRITY of the whole group and hold each other accountable.

231

N-CONCLUSION

L eadership principles are like using a compass or reading a map. Everything relates to where the "N" is and shows you the right direction for your team. For example, when you start the day with **N-COURAGEMENT**, everything else will line up.

Use the *N-COMPASS: Navigating Your Team Forward* book as your compass and starting point.

This book is not only full of leadership examples, but it can also become your:

- **Executive Assistant.** Use *N-Compass* to help you stay focused and on track in building your team, using powerful, positive leadership principles.

- **Daily Devotional.** Use daily for inspiration and encouragement in your personal walk with God.

- **Bible Study Reference Guide.** Use *N-Compass* hand-in-hand as a weekly Bible study and a creative way to make the principles in this book have a lasting impact on your team members.

- **Group Leader's Manual.** Integrate each action point at the end of every *N-Compass* principle to motivate your men's, women's, youth, or leadership group in becoming more proactive in mentoring others.

You are going to be good at something:

Be good at parenting!

Be good at marriage!

Be good at leadership!

Once you find your "N," you will know where you are and which direction to go.

Ready! Set! Go!

LEADERSHIP PRAYER

Heavenly Father,

N-ERGIZE me to **N-SPIRE** my team!

N-VIGORATE me to **N-ABLE** those closest to me!

N-VELOP me with Your power, so they can be **N-UNDATED** with Your ability.

N-HANCE my leadership gifts, so I can **N-STILL** Your **N-TEGRITY** to make my team **N-VINCIBLE**.

Help us **N-JOY** the journey as You **N-RICH** our experience and **N-LIGHTEN** our way with Your **N-COURAGEMENT**.

Make us **N-STRUMENTS** of Your **N-VALUABLE** wisdom and give us **N-COMPARABLE** faith to **N-GAGE** our **N-VIRONMENT**.

Let us be **N-RAPTURED** with Your presence, so that others can **N-COUNTER** Your love.

N-LARGE us to **N-VISION** all that You have for us and **N-TRUST** us to be the **N-TENSE** force of **N-THUSIASTIC** leaders You want us to be.

N-Jesus' name, amen!

SPENCER & CYNDY NORDYKE

From their ministry beginnings with Glory Company, a drama and music team while at Christ for the Nations Institute in Dallas, Texas, to being children's and youth pastors hosting the kids' TV program, Rise & Shine, and Youth WAVE Conventions on satellite to over 1,000 churches across the country, then becoming associate pastors at several major churches, Spencer and Cyndy have always been on the cutting edge of creative ministry, and they wouldn't have it any other way!

Authors of several books, like *Tidal WAVE* and *The Daniel Manual,* they continue to produce ministry tools that help you go further in God.

They have been married over 35 years and have two very talented sons, Jesse and Ryan, with their beautiful daughter-in-laws, and seven wonderful grandchildren.

They travel and minister while writing and developing leadership materials on their journey to fulfill what God has called them to do for this Last Day's revival.

CONTACT

Nordyke Ministries
P. O. Box 1591
Hurst, TX 76053

Office:
817.268.2222

E-Mail:
Cyndy@NordykeMinistries.com

Connect with Us Online:
www. NordykeMinistries.com

Social Media:

To schedule Spencer to speak at your conference or event, call or e-mail us for date availability or visit our website.

To order more resources for your leadership teams, visit our website.

VERSIONS OF THE BIBLE USED